The *Heart* Of Mindfulness-Based Stress Reduction

A MBSR Guide for Clinicians and Clients

Elana Rosenbaum, MS, MSW

Recognized MBSR expert and one of the original instructors
working with Jon Kabat-Zinn, PhD, creator of MBSR

"Lovely emerges as an apt description of this MBSR guidebook written by my dear friend and colleague, Elana Rosenbaum. At heart, Elana is a student – infectiously curious, enduringly fascinated and constantly learning. Together, these qualities make her an exceptional teacher. She is soft, warm and openhearted … and she is fiercely and uncompromisingly alive! Thriving for more than twenty-two years since being diagnosed with cancer and facing multiple reoccurrences, Elana is an embodiment of life itself. Dear reader, be prepared: Entering into this book, you'll catch the fragrance of this fierce, warmhearted aliveness, discovering it as none other than you. L'chaim!"

-Saki F. Santorelli, EdD, MA
Professor of Medicine, Director, MBSR Clinic
Executive Director, Center for Mindfulness in Medicine, Health Care, and Society,
University of Massachusetts Medical School

"This definitive workbook does more than just offer readers an opportunity for their own personal experience of MBSR. From her unique vantage point spanning all the way back to the early days of MBSR, Elana provides a precious window into the wisdom and warmth that continues to bring MBSR to life today. Elana's intuitive presence, playfulness, and heartfulness inspired a generation of MBSR teachers, teaching us all the healing power that arises from bringing kind awareness to our present moment experience. By distilling the core concepts of MBSR within this workbook, Elana not only gives us access to the heart of MBSR; she also shows us a path to open our own."

-Zev Schuman-Olivier, MD
Executive Director, Center for Mindfulness and Compassion Department of Psychiatry,
Cambridge Health Alliance & Harvard Medical School

"Elana Rosenbaum, a master MBSR teacher, has written a gem handbook that provides a practical map and walks us through the nuanced details of the MBSR program. Elana's unique blend of stellar teaching, clinical skills and transformative personal experience with serious illness leads to this clear and comprehensive resource. Written with great wisdom and a light-hearted and compassionate heart, Elana has given us a treasure filled practical tools that will benefit those new to MBSR or experienced teachers, alike."

-Susan Bauer-Wu, PhD, RN
President, Mind & Life Institute
Author of *Leaves Falling Gently: Living with Serious and
Life-Limiting Illness through Mindfulness, Compassion and Connectedness*

"Elana has synthesized important learning themes embedded in the MBSR program. A useful workbook for those interested in developing a mindfulness practice and to reflect on what is important in teaching mindfulness."

-Susan Woods, MSW, LICSW
Senior MBSR/MBCT Advisor, Teacher Trainer and Mentor,
The Mindfulness-Based Professional Training Institute, UC San Diego

This book is dedicated to all who aspire to be mindful and willing to open heart and mind in the service of truth and peace. May we rejoice in the effort and our work bear fruit.

Copyright© 2017 Elana Rosenbaum

Published by:
PESI Publishing & Media
PESI, Inc.
3839 White Ave.
Eau Claire, WI 54703

Cover Design: Amy Rubenzer
Editing: Marietta Whittlesey
Layout: Bookmasters & Amy Rubenzer

Proudly printed in the United States of America
ISBN: 9781683730491

PESI Publishing & Media
www.pesipublishing.com

Table of Contents

Section 4:
Setting the Foundation

Section 5:
Mindful Movement

Section 6:
Examining Stress and Coping Strategies Reacting vs. Responding

Section 7:
Communication

Section 8:
Bringing Mindfulness Home

About the Author

Elana Rosenbaum, MS, MSW, has been integrating mindfulness with psychotherapy and healthcare since 1984. She is one of the original teachers of Mindfulness-Based Stress Reduction (MBSR) at the Center for Mindfulness, working directly with Jon Kabat-Zinn, the founder of MBSR and Saki Santorelli, the current director at the University of Massachusetts Medical School.

Elana is a sought after mindfulness coach, teacher, speaker, workshop leader, meditation retreat leader, and consultant. She has trained thousands in MBSR across the world. She has assisted in the development of mindfulness programs for mental health professionals, social agencies and medical institutions including Dana Farber, and the Mindfulness Training for Primary Care Program at Cambridge Health Alliance, Harvard Medical School. She has been featured in "Chronicle" on CBS and mentioned in many magazine articles including Yoga Journal, Health, Coping, Shambhala Sun and the PBS audio series, "Walking through the Storm."

Her books include, *Here for Now: Living Well with Cancer through Mindfulness* and *Being Well (even when you're sick): Mindfulness Practices for People Living With Cancer and Other Serious Illness.* Elana has a private practice in psychotherapy in Worcester, Massachusetts.

Introduction

I've had the privilege to be associated with Mindfulness-Based stress reduction almost since its beginning. It was around 1981 when I stumbled into a yoga class led by Jon Kabat-Zinn at the University of Massachusetts Medical Center and a meditation session led by Larry Rosenberg. I had no idea at that time that this would initiate a process that would change my life.

I simply wanted to be happier.

I was working as a clinical social worker in a large health maintenance organization and felt burdened and frustrated by the number of people I had to see, the range of problems they presented and the chronic nature of these problems. Nothing seemed to be working, neither my work as a psychotherapist nor my social life. I was approaching 40 and single, and this was not by choice.

Learning that someone at the medical school, a five-minute walk from the HMO where I worked, was offering yoga at lunchtime I went and tried it out. I did the same with the meditation session that was offered at lunch the same week. When I returned to work, I felt rejuvenated and noted increased clarity and calm.

This was the beginning of my mindfulness practice and my entry into MBSR. I saved some money, quit my job at the HMO and opened a private practice. In 1984, I joined Jon and became a teacher working directly with him and Saki Santorelli in the Mindfulness-Based Stress Reduction (MBSR) program at the medical center. I have been involved in this work and practice ever since.

Mindfulness is not mysterious. It is practical. It is more than a set of techniques to add to one's toolbox. It involves personal practice and a willingness to be with our own thoughts and feelings with greater acceptance and less reactivity. What we are embodying as a teacher is as important as what we are teaching.

I discovered the potency of practice when I was diagnosed with cancer in 1995. For years, I had been telling people in my classes that attitude and perspective made a difference in coping with difficulty. In MBSR, a person is trained to feel what they are feeling as it arises noting the thoughts, emotions and sensations, likes and dislikes with a stability of attention that brings acceptance and calm. This brings awareness to the stories and conditioning that influences our ability to manage all the challenges inherent in being human such as illness and loss.

Having cancer and being sick can be exhausting and painful but there are also moments of beauty and love.

My practice helped me be with it all. Teaching MBSR helped me know I was not alone and helped me maintain perspective as I went through chemotherapy and then a stem cell transplant. I have had recurrences. I live with uncertainty and the knowledge that everything changes, but illness has reinvigorated my practice and enhanced my gratitude for the wonders large and small that life brings.

I'd like to convey the essence of MBSR for you in this workbook. We meet our patients as we meet ourselves. Your attitude toward this work makes a difference. Enjoy the journey. It can be fun as well as meaningful. This workbook aims to inspire and provoke reflection as well as introduce you to the program. As you read along let yourself be an explorer who has the courage to enter new territories including the territory of self and love.

Elana Rosenbaum

Section 1

♡

WHAT IS MINDFULNESS–BASED STRESS REDUCTION?

The Origin of MBSR
(Mindfulness-Based Stress Reduction)

The Stress Reduction Program was developed by Jon Kabat-Zinn at the University of Massachusetts Medical Center in 1979. It was born out of Jon's personal meditation practice and his belief as a scientist that the mind/body connection was important and relevant to patient care. The program was created as an adjunct to medicine to teach mindfulness practices, including yoga, to all people regardless of age, vocation or medical condition.

Jon consciously chose to do this in the midst of a busy hospital which he experienced as a magnet for suffering. He purposely designed the mindfulness practices to be presented in everyday language and to be easily understood and applied to daily life. This was radical at the time. Mindfulness was unknown to the medical community or the patients it served. The medical model reigned supreme and its focus was on symptoms. People who needed help were dependent on the expertise of their physician. This was contrary to Jon's belief system, which he wanted to bring to patients to improve their well-being.

Mindfulness-Based stress reduction arose from a confluence of two streams, science and the meditative traditions, both of them central to Jon's life, heart and mind. This is described fully in the article "Some Reflections on the Origins of MBSR, Skillful Means and the Trouble with Maps", *Contemporary Buddhism*. It describes the genesis of MBSR, and its empirical basis that incorporates both the scientific method of observation and investigation into the nature of the mind and the wisdom tradition of Buddhism.

The focus is on experiencing suffering, which is endemic to the human condition. Acknowledging suffering but investigating it with awareness and acceptance, which is mindfulness, creates a path of understanding that is liberating. Suffering is part of the human condition but it need not define us. Depending on intention, attention and attitude it can be alleviated.

Wanting to make mindfulness accessible and not be considered New Age or "flaky" Jon named the program The Stress Reduction and Relaxation Program. Mindfulness was incorporated into the title in the 90s and it became known as Mindfulness-Based Stress Reduction after the efficacy of mindfulness was established and legitimized. MBSR is now considered an evidence-based treatment and is widely researched and practiced.

The philosophical underpinning of MBSR is Buddhist but the program is not Buddhist. "The program is based on universal principles that relate to our humanness and what that means ... *Mindfulness has nothing to do with Buddhism but wakefulness, compassion and wisdom.*" (Kabat-Zinn, 2011). The goal to relieve suffering is universal and applicable to all. A person's belief system is respected, and participants are encouraged to ask questions and discover for themselves the effects of mindfulness and gain insight into the causality of suffering and its release.

Intensive training in mindfulness is core to the program but it is introduced experientially, which is based on a person's direct experience. It is designed to be practical, described plainly and be easy to understand and apply to daily living. Daily practice, consistent effort, and kindness are expected of participants and are integral to being mindful. The aim is personal and societal transformation.

Jon's creation of MBSR came from many sources including the personal. It blends his training at MIT, the hard science of his father, Dr. Elvin Kabat, a scientist renowned for his work in immunology, and his artist mother, Sally. This lent an openness and creativity to his thinking that infuses the program with a fluidity of teaching that is dynamic and interactive.

There is also a precision to instruction and a psycho-educational approach that is sequential and disciplined. Teaching requires flexibility and a responsiveness to class members that is based on active listening and Socratic questioning. Emphasis is on process and self-discovery. The language of the curriculum is in the vernacular, ordinary and easily understood.

Waking up to one's life and what it means to live fully is based on self-discovery and a willingness to observe and be present to one's experience with acceptance as it unfolds in the present moment. The curriculum has changed little since its inception yet change itself and awareness of our relationship to these changes in mind, body and feelings are integral to it. It is expressed through the culture and language of each teacher in their own unique way that makes it authentic and relevant to the population served.

In 2000, Saki Santorelli became the director of The Center for Mindfulness, which includes the stress reduction program, and he has skillfully guided it and expanded its reach throughout the world. He has expanded OASIS Institute, the school for professional teacher education, and has spearheaded its integration into the medical profession, education and corporations. MBSR is now taught in many languages and is applicable to a diversity of people and cultures - and you!

MBSR IS ABOUT AWARENESSING (BEING MINDFUL)

- It is about suffering and its relief.
- It is an active process that engages the whole person in the present moment.
- It is about our common humanity.
- It is relational.
- It is about wondering.
- It cultivates kindness and generosity.
- It cultivates understanding and wisdom.
- It requires courage, commitment, and curiosity.

Threaded throughout each class is respect, authenticity and LOVE

FALSE CONCEPTIONS ABOUT MBSR

1. By attending the sessions my problem or pain will go away.

   Fact: Your relationship to it can change and the pain *may* change but it is not guaranteed. You will gain tools to better understand the situation and understand how your perception of the situation affects "the problem." You may continue to have sensations or experiences that are unpleasant but you will be better equipped to manage them.

2. It's about stopping thoughts or having a blank mind.

   Fact: Thinking is normal. The mind will quiet as acceptance and sustained attention grows, but the aim is enhanced equanimity rather than a blank mind.

3. Mindfulness can only be done at set times.

   Fact: Bringing attention to the present moment with acceptance and kindness is the practice. This is done throughout the day. We practice falling awake rather than falling asleep.

4. Mindfulness is passive.

   Fact: There is an emphasis on non-doing and non-striving, which is about an openness to receive what arises. This requires being awake, alert and non-judgmental which is an active process and takes effort.

5. Mindfulness is about concentration.

   Fact: It is true that concentration is involved but it is only one factor in being mindful. Mindfulness is about awareness and acceptance, awareness of where you place attention and its effect.

6. It is selfish to practice mindfulness and take time for oneself rather than be engaged with others or do chores.

   Fact: This is a common thought as one begins to practice and the long list of have-to-do's arises. In reality, taking the time for the mind to settle lends itself to greater calm and equanimity, which benefits not only the self but also others.

   - Liberation (from suffering) is possible.
   - We are whole. There is more right with us than wrong.
   - We are all connected and inter-dependent.
   - The vehicle for change is awareness.
   - The time is Now!

HOW TO USE THIS BOOK

MBSR needs to be experienced to be understood and evaluated for its efficacy. I recommend experiencing the workbook with two lenses, as a person entering an MBSR class and taking it for the first time and as a possible teacher. It is useful to see how your own reactions and responses influence you in each domain. Stress reduction arises naturally when there is acceptance of life and all its messiness and wonder. The curriculum is awareness. Freedom is the fruit.

You can read the workbook as a series of practices and exercises but, to get the most from it, I recommend doing the meditations on a regular basis as it is done in class. This can be done in addition to your regular practice if you have one, or in place of it. The workbook is designed to give you an overview of the course and provide examples from actual classes that can be used as a guide. Classes are interactive and experiential. The group is an important element of the program but MBSR can also be used individually and adapted to fit specific problem sets and populations.

This workbook is designed to introduce you to the major themes of each class and the reflections and awareness exercises that support these themes. They are for you and your own experiential learning. By understanding them personally, you can more easily understand how they would apply to the population you serve and, if needed, be able to adapt them. For example, if you work with teenagers or children, you'd design mediations that the children can relate to that are shorter and relate to their interests. As you read each section, you can consider its relevance for you and the population you serve. To know this, however, it is important you follow the standard program and the meditations in it so you can experience it first-hand.

Mindfulness is the foundation and its application to daily life is woven throughout each class. Central to every class is the practice of awareness or "awarenessing." Awarenessing means directly experiencing the present moment as a scientist might, with curiosity and an openness that is as free of assumptions and judgment as possible. **It is not about emptying the mind or never having a negative thought. It is about bringing kindness and understanding to the thoughts that are arising and learning about the mind/body connection from them.** Then we can decide for ourselves what maintains stress or contributes to a sense of greater ease. The reflections in this workbook are designed to help you in this process of self-discovery.

There is no formula for "doing" mindfulness; it is about being. MBSR is highly experiential rather than didactic. This workbook is a teaching tool and an entrée into the process of self-discovery. Take your time in reading and answering the questions in the workbook and let yourself experience the themes of each section as they are presented. Be patient with the process and yourself. If you need to set the book aside for a while that is fine but bring awareness to the reasons you are setting it aside (remembering kindness and not being judgmental). When you return to reading the workbook note your intention and its effect.

Everyone is touched by illness, loss and death, teachers and students alike. This is the human condition but how we relate to this is up to us. Happiness, peace, calm and resilience are possible. Of course, this requires practice and commitment to being mindful.

S top
T ake a breath
O pen, observe
P roceed

After many of the exercises, you will be encouraged to stop, take a breath, open to what is arising in body and mind and then proceed. It is marked by the acronym S.T.O.P. and is followed by a self-reflection. It is hoped that this will serve as a reminder for you, the reader, to be able to pause, connect internally to what is arising in body and mind so you can experience directly the power of awareness and its effect on reactivity, which perpetuates stress.

The questions in this workbook are designed to provoke self-examination. Answer them as best you can but don't rush to respond. Letting the question percolate can open new doorways of understanding. The insights you gain are yours and for you alone. At any time, you can S.T.O.P., Stop, Take a breath, Open and Observe and then Proceed. Be curious. Let go of outcomes and expectations. Allow yourself to enter into the unknown and experience the thoughts, feelings and sensations that arise. Have fun and remember the best time to do this is now.

ALLOW YOURSELF TO BE CURIOUS
AND OPEN TO QUESTIONS

> *"Be patient toward all that is unsolved in your heart and try to love the questions themselves, like locked rooms and like books that are now written in a very foreign tongue. Do not now seek the answers, which cannot be given you because you would not be able to live them. And the point is, to live everything. Live the questions now. Perhaps you will then gradually, without noticing it, live along some distant day into the answer."*
>
> — Rainer Maria Rilke

MAKE A COMMITMENT

MBSR classes are interactive and the questions and reflections contained here are designed to help you interact with yourself so you can be your own teacher and student. Journaling can be helpful as you reflect on the questions that arise, and do the worksheets included in each section. The first guided meditation in the MBSR curriculum is a body scan. It begins with, "This is a time for you, a time to be with yourself and to care for yourself . . . a time for self-nurturing . . . don't try too hard to relax, this will just cause tension." This is important to keep in mind as you approach the material in this workbook and your intention in reading it.

To really understand and benefit from the program it is important to commit to do the meditations consistently. Allot yourself enough space and time for practice and reflection. Awareness needs to be cultivated to grow and flourish, and the time you set aside formally for practice will benefit you throughout the day. Old patterns are well established neurologically and psychologically. **Change requires effort and persistence. Sometimes what we find most challenging can bear the greatest fruit.**

As you go through the workbook, remember to acknowledge your effort and accomplishments - and be kind. You'll discover that each meditation will be experienced differently and worksheets can be answered in more than one way and can change over time. Bringing compassion and kindness to yourself as you observe what arises will enhance your capacity to be non-judgmental and witness what arises with greater clarity and equanimity.

See if you can set aside expectations and assumptions so you can observe your own mind/body with a fresh perspective. You'll discover that nothing stays the same. I have been teaching these classes and involved in this work since 1984. I have never been bored. No matter how many times I lead a practice or do an awareness exercise it is never exactly the same. Learning is continual and anew each moment as long as I am truly present. What we learn through our own mindful practice forms the basis for presenting it to others . . . and how we live our lives.

A Mindful Moment

Ask yourself the questions below and let the answers come to you as spontaneously as possible as if you were a scientist entering into the unknown free of expectations, curious and open to discovery.

Where is my attention right now?

_____

_____

_____

What is my experience as I open to this moment—can I observe it as a scientist might with curiosity and an openness to discovery?

_____

_____

_____

What is the position of my body?

_____

_____

_____

What sensations am I experiencing?

_____

_____

_____

What am I hearing?

_____

_____

_____

What am I seeing?

_____

_____

_____

What thoughts am I having?

_____

_____

_____

What am I feeling? How accepting am I of what I am feeling? Is it pleasant, unpleasant or something in between?

_____

_____

_____

This is a mindful moment because you have brought awareness to what is being experienced and you are using all your senses . . . and it is happening now.

It is helpful to have reminders to be in the present. What can help you remember to be here now? How would you use this throughout the day?

_____

_____

_____

WHO TAKES AN MBSR COURSE?

Who doesn't want to feel better, and live with greater ease and balance? Do you? Do you believe that you are already whole, have innate wisdom, the power for transformation and can suffer less? If so, are you feeling this way now? If not, how much do you want this to be the case? What are you willing to do? Would you commit to 31 hours of class time, eight weeks, 2-1/2 to 3 hours once a week, an all-day session on a weekend and about an hour of practice time at home each day? If yes, an MBSR course would be of interest to you. At the time of this writing, more than 24,000 people have completed the MBSR program at the University of Massachusetts Medical Center. People are referred by physicians or come of their own volition. Perhaps they are curious or anxious. They may have heard about the benefits of mindfulness and decided they need to slow down and decrease their stress. Perhaps they have had a heart attack and realize they need to develop a healthier lifestyle. They may be in pain or have a serious medical condition.

People take an MBSR course for all kinds of reasons: anxiety, pain, serious illness or simply to feel better. Ages range from mature adolescent to adults with young children, mid-life and seniors 90+. The population is diverse and comes from all walks of life and economic and social conditions. They do need to be able to understand the language spoken in the class and have the physical capacity to do the guided meditations and awareness exercises. All share a common goal: to gain the tools to experience a greater sense of satisfaction and peace.

Entry into the program is not automatic. It depends on attendance of an orientation session, which is free, and a short interview to determine the sincerity of their commitment and their ability to comply with the program. This means a willingness to take the time to do the meditative practices, which are 45 minutes each, as well as awareness exercises that require daily observation of experiences both pleasant and unpleasant and recording thoughts, feelings, sensations antecedents and outcomes.

Since the program is not didactic but based on direct observation of the workings of one's own mind and body, there must be a capacity for self-observation and reflection. What arises can be revelatory and is challenging to do with persistence, love and openness. One of my teachers joked that the news we find (about ourselves) in meditation may not be good news or news we wanted to know. He laughed when he said this and we laughed with him. He seemed happy, could we? Teaching MBSR is challenging and requires emotional maturity and psychological savvy as well as training in the Mindfulness-Based stress reduction curriculum. People are screened before they enter a class but negative feelings and old traumas can arise.

Research shows that, in fact, we are hard-wired to remember trauma and here in the West we are much more likely to focus on the negative and what is "bad" and not give equal time to what is "good". Of course a person who is psychotic, clinically depressed or has experienced severe trauma and is actively having flash backs might not be appropriate for the program at the Center for Mindfulness. It is important that a person be able to commit to the full eight-week program and not have an ongoing condition that would prevent this. An orientation session is recommended so that each person knows what the expectations for completion are and to optimize compliance. It is important to be aware of our own biases and assumptions. Each person should be evaluated individually. A person's motivation, determination and commitment are key factors in their ability to benefit from the program.

ORIENTATION TO MBSR

The popularity of MBSR has grown exponentially since I began teaching in 1984 and has influenced many Mindfulness-Based interventions such as Mindfulness-Based cognitive therapy for depression, Mindfulness-Based relapse prevention, Mindfulness-Based eating and mindfulness training for primary care doctors and their patients to name a few. Its popularity has led some to see it as a technique that can be easily learned and applied.

MBSR is much more than a series of exercises that can be memorized and applied. There is a wholeness to it that leads a person to develop greater awareness and acceptance. It is not easy to take 45-60 minutes each day to stop and listen to a guided meditation that requires sustained attention and highlights how we view the world. This can take determination and hardiness. Not everyone can do or is willing to do this. Expectations can be unrealistic. Some think of it as a quick and easy cure for what ails them; others may not have the will or the ability to take time each day to stop and formally practice mindfulness.

The program is experiential and requires active participation rather than passive learning. As a person sits quietly, strong emotions can arise and it is important to be able to tolerate strong feelings without being flooded or re-traumatized. So that expectations are realistic about this rigorous, 31-hour program that requires an hour of daily home practice, The Center for Mindfulness holds a free orientation session. People are given a taste of the program, led in some short meditations and briefly screened as to appropriateness for entry.

Recommendations for exclusion:

- Anyone who is not willing to commit to participating fully in all classes and complying with the daily mindfulness practices.
- A person who has a current, non-remitting, alcohol or illicit drug use disorder or poses an imminent risk of suicide or danger to self or others or is intoxicated with alcohol or drugs during class.
- A person who displays symptoms of psychosis, thought disorder, and/or severe mental illness.
- Anyone who does not have the interpersonal skills to tolerate being a group member.

It is important to be sensitive to cultural differences and confirm full understanding of the above. If there is any question of appropriateness it is important to get consent to speak to the person's doctor or therapist and gain further information on their condition and ability to benefit from the class.

Risks, benefits and possible side effects*
Risks:
- Seeing something about yourself you don't like.
- Change. You could change.
- Change requires adjustments to regain a sense of balance.
- You might notice ways in which you are not balanced.
- You might experience feelings of pain.
- You might experience feelings of joy.

- You can get to know yourself better; insight can come without warning.
- Old memories could return.
- You'll probably have to readjust your schedule to do the homework.
- You'll have to let some things go.
- You'll be facing the unknown - yourself.
- Relationships, both with yourself and others, might be experienced differently.
- You might not like what you discover.
- You will be challenged.
- You could be freer; that means more choices.

Benefits:

- Less mental anguish.
- A greater sense of well-being.
- Happiness, joy, peace.
- A greater sense of balance in your life.
- Mindfulness: Clear seeing and understanding.
- A quieter mind.
- A sense of wholeness, vastness, space, connection.

Possible Side Effects:

- New understanding.
- A more expansive perspective.
- Wonder fullness.

Life is filled with risks, benefits and side effects. I've signed the consent form. If you want to be fully alive, is there another choice?

*Excerpt from *Here For Now: Living Well with Cancer through Mindfulness,* (Rosenbaum, 2005)

WHAT IS SUFFERING?

Core to MBSR is the relief of suffering. Suffering is universal, but each person experiences it uniquely. There are many sources of suffering but under each of these causes is a sense of danger and a threat to the self. Wanting things to be different than they are and resisting the reality of one's experience can cause suffering. There can be craving, grasping and holding on to what cannot be held: a recipe for misery. Often it is below our level of awareness. A challenge to practice is facing our own humanness, the self that suffers as well as feels joy. When things go well they can be ignored and taken for granted. Pain rivets attention. Being able to meet this pain, emotional and physical, and lean into it with love is one of the goals of MBSR.

Mindfulness does not prevent death, loss or illness. Bad things happen BUT how we relate to them internally and externally makes a difference. Many people equate mindfulness with emptying the mind rather than accepting the ways of the mind. Acceptance is not automatic. It is a process and takes practice. Compassion, patience and kindness are needed to maintain awareness and continue to practice mindfulness.

Bringing awareness to the moment with kindness and compassion enlivens heart and mind. It allows us to really enter into our experience as it is fully. We may notice the blooming of a flower that we might have otherwise overlooked, or the wonder of having indoor plumbing and the feel of water touching our skin and the freshness that ensues. It helps us soften into pain and meet fear rather than push it away and discover what is possible rather than fixate on future or past.

A person attending a workshop I was giving on MBSR came up to me after it was over. She said she came thinking mindfulness was not for her; it was too hard. She experienced a lot of anxiety and had high expectations for herself and how she *should be and what should happen.* When she wasn't anxious, she worried about being anxious and having an anxiety attack. It was crippling and invaded her days. There was a lot of judgment and with it suffering.

As we went through the day of the workshop, pausing, breathing, smiling, she discovered she did have control. She could pause. She could feel her body, feel her feet, experience her breath and refocus her attention. *It became possible to not only focus on anxiety.* During the sensory awareness exercise, eating a raisin mindfully, she felt the explosion of flavor in her mouth and experienced the object (raisin) being transformed. Entering into the present helped make her world bigger than her thoughts and her fears. It enabled her to feel anxiety as sensation without panicking. She realized she could watch her thoughts rather than react to them.

Kindness, compassion and acceptance are central to this process as is curiosity and repeated practice. Anxiety did not disappear fully but the suffering around it decreased and it was more manageable. Experiencing mindfulness directly took it from an intellectual exercise that was conceptual and easy to misunderstand, to a practical level that demonstrated change was possible and with it relief from suffering.

SUFFERING

Most suffering is caused by wishing things were different than they are. What would you like to be different than it is? Please describe it as fully as possible and what makes it difficult to accept. As you bring it to mind what do you feel in your body?

_____

_____

_____

What thoughts do you have about it? How often? How long do they last?

_____

_____

_____

What is the effect of these thoughts in your body?

_____

_____

_____

How does it shape your behavior?

_____

_____

_____

S.T.O.P.

Stop
Take a breath
Open, observe
Proceed

I. Stop. Take a breath. Open and Observe. Proceed.

- Look around you.
- Feel your feet on the ground.
- Listen to any sounds that are here.
- Are you on an in-breath or out-breath?
- Can you feel the rhythm of your breath moving and changing?
- Where in your body do you feel the breath?
- How accepting can you be of what is being felt NOW?
- In this moment is there suffering? If so, what is it?

Liberation/relief from suffering

What does it mean to experience a sense of liberation, relief from suffering?

_____

_____

Do your best to imagine yourself experiencing this freedom.

_____

_____

How do you picture it influencing the work you do and how you are living now? Please describe it as best you can including:

_____

_____

Thoughts:

_____

_____

_____

Feelings:

_____

_____

_____

Sensations:

_____

_____

_____

If you like, you can even draw or find an image that represents this state.

SETTING INTENTION

Intention is powerful. Remembering what we truly want and forming realistic goals, without striving or pushing so hard that we create stress is part of being mindful. Committing to bringing awareness to our thoughts, our feeling and sensations all the time can be a struggle. We have to trust it's possible to be happier, healthier and live with greater ease even in the midst of illness and loss.

If we judge ourselves negatively, which is common, aversion arises which reinforces our defenses and the cycle of suffering. The more we truly want to suffer less and connect to the deep desire for enhanced well-being the easier it is to be mindful. Then we can pay attention to how we are living our life and the consequences of our thoughts, feelings and actions.

Change begins with awareness and acceptance of our own foibles, our humanness. Continuing to bring awareness to what arises requires commitment, patience and trust - "everything passes" is a favorite phrase, as is "I'm human." Can we be curious about the workings of our mind and the adventure of being human? How do we approach what we observe inside us and around us? Are we fearful, can we bring compassion to ourselves as we open to all the workings of our mind and use what we don't like to cultivate healthier modes of being? Are we willing to question established ways of being? Are we open to new learning? Can we find it interesting or does the effort feel too hard?

MY INTENTION

What do you want to gain by reading this book - really!?

Thomas Merton, a famous Christian writer, theologian and mystic believed that we already have the capacity within us to be at peace and live in harmony with ourselves and others. What do you believe? What do you seek? How does it influence your intention?

Allow yourself to get into a comfortable position in a place where you will not be disturbed. Take some time to experience your body and feel the breath as you breathe noting where you feel it most plainly. Take a few minutes to settle in and then ask yourself each of the questions below, taking your time and doing one at a time. No rushing, striving or trying to make something happen.

Allowing each question to be like a pebble dropped into a pond ask it to yourself repeatedly. Don't overthink the answer but allow responses to come to you spontaneously. Not having an answer can itself be informative. You can imagine your question being like the pebble and, as it falls deeper and deeper into the pond, your response deepens and becomes more known to you. Then write it down, read it, pause, and do it again.

What do I really want for myself? What is my deepest desire?

_____

_____

_____

How am I living now and what am I doing to fulfill this desire?

_____

_____

_____

What is needed to fulfill this desire?

_____

_____

_____

What obstacles may I have to overcome to fulfill this desire?

_____

_____

_____

What qualities do I need to cultivate or strengthen to thrive and experience what is desired?

_____

_____

_____

ALLOW YOURSELF TO FORM AN INTENTION and COMMIT TO THE INTENTION.

Take some time to contemplate what you have written and ask yourself again what is really important and meaningful to you and then write down your intention.

My intention is _____

Remember: Intention is the engine that drives us. It is not always conscious, but it influences our focus of attention and how we live our lives. For example, if the intention is to be kind and compassionate, when we notice ourselves being judgmental and critical it will help us remember that this is conditioning and it will be easier to be accepting of what transpires. The intention to be kind and not judgmental can also help us maintain perspective and remember that everything changes. This will help us persevere and continue to practice mindfulness.

What will support your intention - inside yourself?

_____

_____

_____

What will support your intention - outside yourself?

_____

_____

_____

Imagine yourself fulfilling your intention and jot down what that is and how it affects the way you are living. It is easy to forget to meditate, so commitment is needed - like the postman - in good weather or bad. The commitment is not to the teacher or an authority figure but to ourselves.

WILLINGNESS/COMMITMENT

How willing am I to S.T.O.P. each day and take the time to practice Mindfulness? Please write down what you think it will involve and how you plan to maintain its practice.

_____

_____

_____

_____

My commitment is

_____

_____

_____

_____

Practice time(s)

_____

_____

_____

_____

Practice place(s)

_____

_____

_____

_____

Section 2

WHAT IS MINDFULNESS?

Mindfulness:
A Way of Being

> *"Only that day dawns to which we are awake."*
> — Henry David Thoreau

WHAT DOES IT MEAN TO BE MINDFUL?

MEANING AND PURPOSE

The present moment is our home. I think of mindfulness with a capital M, which refers to the way we are living and the principles that inform us. This includes behaving morally and cultivating qualities such as generosity, openness, kindness, non-striving, a beginner's mind and acceptance. Acknowledging our experience as it unfolds and the way we pay attention is not only to develop concentration but a practice in patience, trust and being non-judgmental. By viewing what arises with discernment and discrimination and with the eyes of a person experiencing our object of attention as if it were the first time, we are cultivating a fresh perspective. This leads to greater choices.

Mindfulness is a practice of awareness and being rather than doing. It is a translation from the Pali word "sati" which in is often translated as awareness. This includes the process of remembering or re-collecting, bringing together what we think as separate to experiencing the wholeness of life. This is an active and ongoing process and the gerund awarenessing was coined by Kabat-Zinn to reflect this dynamic process.

Kabat-Zinn defines mindfulness as paying attention on purpose in a particular way to the present moment non-judgmentally.

On Purpose: With intention and commitment

To the present moment: By directly experiencing each moment as it arises moment by moment.

Without Judgment: By accepting and being with what is present rather than resisting what is being directly experienced.

John Milton in *Paradise Lost* writes, "The mind can make a Heaven of Hell and a Hell of Heaven." In other words, the mind is powerful. Observing the workings of the mind helps us experience directly the way it is leading us. The unconscious becomes conscious and insight penetrates mistaken beliefs and harmful actions. Rather than blocking, denying or fighting what arises, we acknowledge it. In Mindfulness-Based cognitive therapy, it is said:

You don't have to like it but you do need to acknowledge it.

There is an ethical basis to mindfulness. We practice in the service of greater harmony, clarity and wisdom. By promising to do no harm and benefit ourselves and all others, the mind cleanses itself. Over time (and struggle) there is a purification. Insight penetrates mistaken beliefs and concepts and we get to know and learn the consequences of our thoughts, feelings and actions. We pay attention with the intention to harness the power of the mind to experience greater harmony, clarity and wisdom.

Harmony, Clarity, and Wisdom - When we are able to open with acceptance to what is true, we become peaceful and free from habits that do not contribute to well-being, and focus on what is wholesome and beneficial.

This takes practice and commitment.

Practice and Commitment are essential to Mindfulness!

When we commit ourselves to being awake and bringing awareness (mindfulness) into our lives, the ordinary is experienced more fully. Thich Nhat Hahn has a gatha, a short poem, that he introduces to beginning meditators. It is . . .

"Breathing in I calm body and mind
Breathing out I smile.
Dwelling in the present moment.
It is a precious moment."

Realizing we are alive brings perspective to what is being experienced. You can use this *gatha* at any time. It plants the seeds of peace and is helpful in maintaining perspective when we encounter difficulties.

To Consider: What words would you use to define mindfulness? If you were to explain it to another what would you highlight? In what ways might your description differ in order to match the language and understanding of the population you serve?

Stop
Take a breath
Open, observe
Proceed

BREATHING SPACE

Put down the book for a moment, close your eyes and let yourself experience the breath moving your body. If you like, on the inhale say "calm" and on the exhale "release". Allowing the muscles of your face to relax and noticing what arises as you do this. If you like, you can smile and bring awareness to how this affects your experience. Is it helpful in observing what arises without judgment or trying to change it.

What do you observe as you do this? Without saying calm but giving full attention to the breath note how it moves your body and what comes into your attention. You can bring awareness to the muscles of your face but no need to consciously smile. When you notice your attention is not in the present moment and has wandered away from your experiencing what arises remember, come home to breath. Remember your intention and let yourself be curious. What happens?

When you begin reading again has anything changed? Can you appreciate this moment as precious? Write down what you experienced:

Sensations:

_____

_____

Feelings and Emotions noting pleasant, unpleasant or neutral:

_____

_____

Thoughts:

_____

_____

A BREATHING SPACE

Throughout the day, stop and take a moment to observe what you are experiencing in body, mind and feelings.

Consciously feel the breath moving in your body . . .

Observe . . .

Allow . . .

Proceed . . .

EVERYTHING CHANGES – IMPERMANENCE

You may have noticed by now that nothing stays the same. Everything changes. As you feel your breath, you can bring awareness to the uniqueness of each breath. Each one is slightly different yet there is a continuity of flow that responds to both internal and external events. By paying attention with the intention to learn and observe the effect of our thoughts, feelings and actions free of judgment, we are freer to evaluate whether they are serving us in a wholesome healthy manner or not.

The first instruction in practicing mindfulness is to be aware of what is here and to let it be rather than rush to do something to change it. By allowing and leaning into what arises with gentleness and care it is possible to investigate causes and conditions and gather information so that we can find our balance even in the midst of a turbulent change—and then we have choices as to how to proceed.

MBSR trusts the innate wisdom within each of us and our own capacity for transformation. This means acknowledging impermanence: everything changes. Aging, illness, loss and death are part of the human condition. When something bad happens, it is good to know it will change, when something good happens we want to hold onto it but cannot. Accepting how our own conditioning and mental formations add or hinder our ability to be resilient and to thrive is based on an acceptance of impermanence. Recognizing this and bringing awareness to our response to change is part of being mindful and is core to the MBSR curriculum.

MY RELATIONSHIP TO CHANGE

Take a few minutes and simply rest in the moment bringing awareness to the position of your body and the breath entering it, noting where you feel it, and leaving. As you do so, allow yourself not to change it in any way but note the uniqueness of each one. Are they of even lengths? Is one longer or shorter than another? How quickly or slowly do they move? Does this change? Then bring your attention to sound. What do you hear? How does that change?

After you do this for a few minutes open your eyes. Is there anything that you observe as different from before? What? How have you changed? Is your position the same as earlier? What about breath? Thoughts? Sensations? Note your response.

Change forces a person to adapt and come to a new balance. It often creates stress. What is your relationship to change? Some changes can be very dramatic and finding peace within them can be challenging. When I was ill, I found that words were often inadequate in expressing what I thought and how I felt. I found that letting images form on paper very helpful. The watercolor below emerged to remind me that peace was possible and change is a part of life. It gives me a sense of ocean and sky that I find calming. The words also arose spontaneously and helped me be more accepting of my condition.

Are there any images that you have or would like to create that represent mindfulness and serve to bring greater peacefulness? You may name them or illustrate on a piece of paper.

THE USE OF STORY

When we experience the feeling of breathing in and out, we are experiencing change but often we take this miracle of life for granted. To emphasize the transitory nature of things and approach this subject in a right-brained way, I sometimes tell the story of Solomon's ring.

Solomon, who is reputed to have been very wise, likes to surround himself with people in his retinue who are also kind and generous as well as wise and trustworthy. One of his ministers was very smart but not very kind and was so puffed up with his own position and learnings that he was quite arrogant. He thought he could never fail in any task. Solomon, wanting to teach him a lesson in humility, decided he'd ask him to do something for him that was impossible to achieve. To this effect Solomon called the minister into his throne room and asked,

"Can you bring me a ring that can make a happy person sad and a sad person happy?"

The minister, thrilled that the king had selected him to do a personal favor, replied, *"Oh yes, Your Majesty. Right away."*

Solomon, wanting to teach him a lesson but not prolong the time needed for this, said,

"It doesn't have to be right away but I'd like it within three days."

The minister left the throne room and immediately went to his favorite jeweler and demanded a ring that would make a happy person sad and a sad person happy.

With fear and trembling, the jeweler informed the minister he did not have such a ring. In a rage, the minister went to another shop and got a similar response. This continued with the minister becoming more and more desperate and unhappy as he went from place to place, even asking family and friends if they had such a ring. No one could help him.

At the end of the third day feeling very sad and much less sure of himself, he trudged slowly toward the palace with heavy heart. Just as he was about to approach the entrance to the palace he saw a peddler who had never been there before. Thinking he'd try one more time, he went toward the stall where brass rings were displayed and asked in a soft, respectful tone for such a ring. The peddler took pity on him and seeing the sincerity of his request replied,

"Yes, I think I can help you."

He then selected a ring and wrote something inside it and gave it to the minister. Seeing it and reading the inscription the minister smiled and felt lighter and happier. He proceeded into the palace and found Solomon in the midst of a great feast with many happy people all dancing to wonderful music and eating the delicious and plentiful food. Solomon surrounded by beautiful women and the richness of his surroundings was enjoying himself very happily. The minister approached him, knelt down and, without his usual arrogance or bluster, presented the ring to the king. Upon reading the inscription, Solomon's countenance changed and as he looked around, he experienced sadness.

What do you think was written on the ring? Some guess, often there is silence. After a period of time I give the answer.

"This too shall pass"

THIS TOO SHALL PASS

1. What in your life makes you happy? Jot it down. Noting thoughts, feelings (pleasant, unpleasant, neutral), sensations.

   _____

   _____

2. Imagine it passing and as you do so note:
   Thoughts about it passing

   _____

   _____

   What is felt in the body

   _____

   _____

   Thoughts in the mind

   _____

   _____

   Feelings

   _____

   _____

3. What in your life makes you sad? Jot it down. Noting thoughts, feelings (pleasant, unpleasant, neutral), sensations.

   _____

   _____

4. Imagine it passing. Note what is felt in your body as you bring into awareness the sadness passing.

   What thoughts are present?

   _____

   What feelings are present?

   _____

   What sensations are present?

   _____

EXPERIENCING CONNECTION

Mindfulness is a way of being that encompasses our common humanity and the realization that we are all connected to each other. Often in the first class of MBSR people are surprised to learn that they are not alone. Every person there wants something to change and to be different from what it is. Their "problem" looms large and often defines their sense of self.

As we go around the room and people state why they are taking the program, there is a realization that they are not alone. Heads nod in agreement as people share why they have come to the class.

There are always both women and men who suffer from anxiety. It is a relief for them to name it. Sometimes in the beginning as we go around the circle, people say their names, and why they have come, there is a stiffness, a shyness, but as people hear each other's reasons for attending, the room warms and it becomes easier to be honest and allow vulnerability and pain to show.

Friendships are formed and there is a sense of possibility. Problems vary, but people's willingness to self-disclose why they are taking MBSR is very moving and creates trust and bonding. It is a relief to not have to pretend all is fine or mask one's true feelings. In this release, mindfulness grows and peace begins.

ALLOWING VULNERABILITY GROWS PEACE
MINDFULNESS IS R's (Ours):

- Remember - To Be Mindful . . .
- Return - To The Present Moment
- Recognize - What Is True
- Realize - Everything Changes
- Release - What No Longer Serves Us
- Refocus - On The Here And Now
- Recover - Our Balance
- Regain - Perspective
- Replenish
- Rest - Restore - Renew

Introducing Mindfulness

Describe mindfulness in your own words and based on your experience. You can write it down and say it to yourself. When ready, introduce mindfulness to another person first in words and then through a short experience of mindfulness.

To facilitate connection bring awareness to your body position and where you are in relation to the person you are instructing. Note the rhythm of your breath and whether there is a synchronization between it and that of the person you are instructing. **A calm and steady demeanor is contagious. Your voice, tone and pacing are important.**

If there is anxiety in the person you are teaching and you note breath is shallow and rapid, speaking slowly, breathing evenly and matching words to breath can lead a person to a calmer, more even pattern of breathing. Remember to be inviting and allowing so you are encouraging the ability to witness what arises without judgment.

Take your time. Let go of YOUR expectations of how you think the person should respond. Be aware of shifts of attention and changes in breathing pattern.

Follow the lead of the person you are instructing so you can join with them and guide them to an open calm awareness that is based on direct experience as it occurs in the present. Feel free to pause and check in with yourself, as well as the person you are instructing.

Practice connecting and being present to your partner as you help them bring attention to their experience as it unfolds in the present moment. If you like, you can have them feel their breath, listen to sounds or look around the room, whatever feels best at the time. You can do this more than once. Your non-verbal behavior and your attitude are as important as the words you choose to define mindfulness.

Note what arises in you (thoughts, feelings, sensations) as you do this. When you are finished, feel free to ask how it was for the person you were instructing in mindfulness. Let this be a partnership, a joint journey of discovery that is based in the here and now. Note your expectations and see if you can approach this with curiosity and wonder rather than having a fixed outcome in mind.

Write what you have learned by doing the above. I recommend doing this more than once and with different people.

CORE ATTITUDES IN BEING MINDFUL

To open to the present moment and truly experience it as present is not automatic. I am lucky; having experienced a serious illness, I know I will die. It is not conceptual but a fact. When I was very sick, each moment was special. Once I began feeling better and returned to a more normal routine, it was easy to forget how precious it was to be breathing, walking, talking and able to take care of myself and engage in the routines of daily living.

We are wired to experience threats to our well-being, and it is easy to take for granted what we already have within us and around us. Part of being mindful is remembering that it OK to dwell in the present moment and to allow the mind to settle and to be, rather than to do. It is easy to forget that we are human beings not human doings.

In *Full Catastrophe Living*, Jon Kabat-Zinn lists seven core attitudes that are intrinsic to mindfulness. They are:

- Non-judging
- Patience
- Beginner's mind
- Trust
- Non-striving
- Acceptance
- Letting-go

These attitudes are threaded throughout the eight weeks of the course, along with compassion and kindness.

CORE ATTITUDES IN PRACTICING MINDFULNESS

- Non-judging
- Patience
- Beginner's mind
- Trust
- Non-striving

- Acceptance
- Letting-go
- Compassion
- Kindness

Core Attitudes

NON-JUDGING

This is the ability to bring awareness to directly experience the moment free of bias. We often want things to be different than they are and are critical of ourselves for not being how we *think we should be*. This causes suffering. Being judgmental is different than evaluating and discerning what is correct. It is often interpreted as being critical and has a negative connotation and interferes with clarity and acceptance (which relieve suffering).

Describe what being non-judgmental means to you.

What is an example of a common judgment that you could acknowledge and release?

_____

_____

_____

Reflection: Notice when judgment arises - of another person, of yourself. Remember not to judge your judging.

PATIENCE

Changing well-established behaviors and attitudes that have become habits is not easy. Neural pathways have been formed that become our default position and are often automatic and unconscious. Creating new pathways requires repetition and continual effort. Patience eases this process.

What does this mean for you?

_____

_____

_____

Written Reflection: What are you doing or think you should be doing that requires patience? Write about it.

_____

_____

_____

BEGINNER'S MIND

The more we can be aware of our expectations and assumptions, the freer we can be to evaluate their veracity and enter into the moment with the freshness of a child discovering the world with curiosity as if it were the first time.

In your own words, please describe what it is to have a beginner's mind.

_____

_____

_____

Choose an object that is familiar and study it for a few minutes as if you've never seen it before. What can you discover? Write about it. Can you imagine a familiar person or situation that you could see with a fresh perspective?

_____

_____

_____

TRUST

If we allow ourselves to not know what the future will bring, we can enter into each moment anew with a sense of freedom from the past. This requires trusting the process of awarenessing itself and allowing the unknown to be discovered in the present.

What does trust mean to you?

Reflection: Bring some awareness to a time that you trusted your intuition and acted from an inner knowing and surety. How does it feel in your body as you reflect on this? Write it down. What thoughts, if any, are present when you experience this inner sense of trust?

_____

_____

_____

NON-STRIVING

Trying to force something to happen or to make it be different than it is causes contraction and stress. Letting be and receiving what is present creates relaxation and new possibilities.

Definition: How do you experience striving in your life? What is its effect? What do you think would happen if you had a more relaxed attitude about it?

_____

_____

_____

Exercise/Reflection: In your meditation, bring awareness to any manipulation of breath or a pushing for something to happen or be different from what is being experienced. How do you experience "letting-be" rather than doing?

_____

_____

_____

Non-doing seems to go against our doing culture. Let yourself put down this book and give yourself permission to do nothing for one minute. You can time it if you like. After a minute, describe what this experience was like.

_____

_____

_____

ACCEPTANCE

Peace comes when we can simply be with our direct experience and accept/acknowledge what is occurring as it is occurring, as a scientist might - as free of judgment as possible. Nothing can change unless we first acknowledge what is present and meet it with an open heart and mind.

What does acceptance mean to you? Can you define it?

_____

_____

_____

What allows for acceptance of difficult feelings?

_____

_____

_____

How does acceptance manifest in your life, personally and professionally?

_____

_____

_____

LETTING-GO

Everything changes. Recognizing impermanence is part of being mindful. You can contain water but you can't hold on to it. Each moment is unique unto itself. Holding on to it is impossible and when we try to do so, we are creating suffering rather than learning how to find our balance within change and develop resiliency.

Letting go does not have to be volitional. It happens naturally as we breathe. Without doing anything, one breath follows another, one leaves and the other follows. Change is unavoidable but it is often resisted, which creates stress. We tend to want to hold onto the good and push away what we consider to be bad. Can you think of something that you are holding onto to about yourself that no longer serves you? Write it down.

_____

_____

_____

Can you imagine letting it go? Note how it feels to do so?

_____

_____

_____

KINDNESS AND COMPASSION

Kindness is needed not only toward others but also to ourselves. What arises in the mind can be difficult to accept and painful to experience. We need to be able to embrace our foibles and acknowledge our vulnerability, holding ourselves tenderly as we might a small child. Awareness encompasses compassion and care. Our hearts break open in recognition of suffering and the desire to relieve it.

There are many small kindnesses we may give and receive without recognition. It can be kind to give a helping hand or to smile. Write down some ways that you have been kind to another and they to you.

_____

_____

_____

What are the thoughts and feelings that accompany the experience of kindness? How do you incorporate kindness into your day? Write down specific times and ways you are kind to yourself. What is its effect?

_____

_____

_____

REFLECTION ON ATTITUDES

Let's take a few minutes to reflect on the attitudes inherent in mindfulness beginning by putting the book down and bringing awareness to your body and the position it is in now. If you can, I recommend coming to a sitting position that is upright, pelvis slightly forward, head and spine in alignment so chin is level with the floor. If you are sitting in a chair, let your hands rest on your lap or your thighs and have your legs uncrossed and feet flat on the floor. If you are using a cushion, you can sit in a lotus position with your legs crossed and one foot resting on the thigh of the opposite leg putting a cushion under it for support if needed, or sit upright with one leg inside the other. You can also kneel resting your buttock on a cushion with your legs on either side of you.

Once you are in a stable position, you can bring attention to your breath noticing each in-breath as it arrives and out-breath as it goes. Allow yourself to have the breath be your major focus of attention and anchor to the present.

Have no agenda but to give yourself three minutes to simply rest your attention here in the present moment and experience your body being breathed. As you do so, you'll notice your attention moving away from the breath.

Recommit to staying present. If you are feeling pain, do your best to experience it as sensation and breathe softly into it and with it. When you return to the breath as your primary object of attention, note whether it is an inhalation or exhalation that you are feeling.

Note what it is for you to be present with awareness for these three minutes. Do any attitudes arise that you would like to add to the list? If so, feel free to include them in this meditation.

The attitudes I observed in this meditation are:

_____

_____

_____

Attitudes I'd like to cultivate are:

_____

_____

_____

Section 3

EMBODYING MINDFULNESS

Being a Mindfulness-Based Stress Reduction Teacher

When I am leading a workshop on Mindfulness-Based stress reduction, I always ask, *"why are you here?"* I know people come to get continuing education credits and I acknowledge that this will be achieved if they stay for the eight hours of the day but I ask again, *"what would you really like to receive today?"*

Answers vary, but all come for personal as well as professional reasons. Some have familiarity with mindfulness while others do not, but universally there is a hunger for inspiration and nourishment. The work we do in caring for others is hard and can be very fatiguing. Often it is easier to care for others rather than the self and to externalize difficulties rather than investigate our own relationship to them. Blame for our stress is directed towards other people or situations, rather than focusing on our response to it. MBSR is very interactive, but it is based on the premise that to help others we must begin with our own learning. Rabbi Hillel, a famous Jewish religious leader, sage and scholar of the 11th century, wrote in *Ethics of the Fathers* 1:14, *"If I am not for myself, who will be? If I am only for myself what am I? If not now, when?"* **The ability to teach others begins with ourselves. Once one commits to awarenessing it becomes part of everyday life and impacts every moment we are here.**

Mindfulness is a practice that has a long history and is part of a tradition that originated with the Buddha over a thousand years ago. Here in the West we tend to want quick fixes. The Buddha, which means awakened one, was a man of his time and a careful observer of human behavior. It took many years of study and experimentation for him to discover the roots of suffering and free himself from it. In my beginning years as a teacher, I suffered because I thought that in order to help others I needed to be perfect and liberated, like the Buddha after he was liberated, not as he was struggling to learn and cope with his demons, greed, hatred and delusion. This created suffering.

Introducing mindfulness to others and teaching mindfulness in a program that is Mindfulness-Based requires an ongoing personal practice and involves training. One can want to be a good teacher who is fully awake and open, but self-consciousness and fear can get in the way.

When I began to do this work, worrying about my performance interfered with my ability to be present and kept me in my head with a false ideal rather than with the participants in the room with me. There is a curriculum to follow in MBSR and it is important how it is conveyed. It cannot be done unless it is delivered with an authenticity that comes from personal experience. All of the training programs at The Center for Mindfulness begin with personal practice. This means acknowledging our humanness, our foibles and our strengths. How we relate to the self and our conditioning, our willingness to engage with our selves, what we appreciate and what we wish were different affects how we teach mindfulness.

Mindfulness-Based stress reduction values the dignity of the human being and sees its teachers as a vehicle embodying and maintaining these standards. Teachers are both shepherd and flock. There is a recognition that we are all in the same boat, traveling on the same sea as the people who come to us for help. Do no harm and be a benefit to all beings is a core teaching. There is a commitment to being aware of our actions and their effect.

Just as we urge others to be kind and non-judgmental in observing the workings of their minds, thoughts, feelings and sensations, we teachers do the same. This means admitting mistakes, acknowledging vulnerability, maintaining an open and flexible awareness, being patient and listening to self and others with respect. Trust is needed to do this, even faith; that awareness is liberating. Acknowledging what is true helps it be less onerous and sticky. There is less me, more us, less story and more direct observation of experience that is based on clarity and understanding.

This requires intention and commitment, effort and a good sense of humor. A beginner's mind is needed that is open to discovery and fresh perspectives. Kindness and compassion are core values and we need to remember to **not** be self-blaming and critical when we become aware of our own obstacles to peace. Bringing awareness and acceptance to our own anger, our doubts, our fears, our delusions, our wanting things to be different than they are, our wanting to hold on to the pleasant and push away the unpleasant is the curriculum. MBSR allows us to see and to know our humanness and, in so doing, be transformed.

Facing our humanness and believing that what we do and feel contributes to a life of greater peace. This is not automatic or simple. For example, a man in one of our MBSR classes came because he wanted to improve his family life. When asked to examine what caused him stress and to keep a record of unpleasant feelings, thoughts and sensations he said, "I have none. When I get angry, I yell. I like to yell and it relieves stress."

Upon inquiry, it was discovered that he did not bring awareness to what happened before, during or after he yelled. He didn't want to know the feelings, thoughts or physical sensations that accompanied his anger. A core value was family stability and harmony. To be in alignment with this value, he'd need to look at the effect of his yelling and decide whether it fostered harmony or worked against it. Was he willing to examine this further or could he be content with continuing to yell and its consequences?

Seeing the connection between his behavior and what ensued was liberating. Valuing harmony, he began to recognize feelings other than anger and learned more ways to manage his stress. I will talk more about some of these coping strategies in a later chapter.

EMBODYING MINDFULNESS

Learning MBSR is a process that takes time and effort as well as practice. It is learned not just by the head but also the heart. Our body reflects this living practice in our non-verbal communication and shapes how the material is conveyed. We must genuinely practice mindfulness ourselves to know the material and be able to convey it to others. How we relate to our own aversions, how much we are willing to bring attention to our cravings, our hatreds and our delusions affects our connection to others and how we can help those who come to us.

To do this work we must be willing to face ourselves and lean into rather than shy away from what we don't like or wish was different than it is. It is also good to have teachers, supervisors and colleagues who can give us honest feedback on our work.

A mindfulness teacher, like the participants in an MBSR course, deepens her/his ability to stop and recognize what is arising with clarity, love, kindness and equanimity. I think of the teacher as a shepherd tending and caring for her or his flock and using the fire of attention for learning. We may have heard about mindfulness, see our friends practicing it and believe in its benefits, but even with the best intentions, it requires a steady resolve. This is why it is helpful to have a supportive community.

As we sit quietly with ourselves and open to the workings of mind/heart/body, there is a need to be courageous as we face our own attitudes, thoughts and behaviors. Rather than shy away from difficulty and pain, there is a need to persevere. Resolve must be strong and, with it, kindness and compassion.

REQUIRED FOR TEACHING

- Knowing how your practice is being lived and manifests in your daily life
- A willingness to be in the fire and have the courage to be authentic, curious and make mistakes
- The ability to be flexible and maintain perspective
- Opening to a lifelong adventure of discovery
- A willingness to remember again and again to be present and open
- Remembering what brings you to this work
- A desire to be of service and benefit other and yourself
- A willingness to receive feedback and learn from mistakes
- Realizing our inter-connectedness and our common humanity
- Kindness

WHAT MBSR IS ABOUT

It is always useful to examine why we are doing what we are doing and discover the value it represents for us. To highlight the meaning of learning about MBSR and practicing mindfulness, I asked a group of people engaged in this process of learning what they thought the program was about. With great enthusiasm words popped out, "wonder, act of love, wholeness, home, connection, vulnerability-allowing and opening to it, common humanity, etc."

These words came from their personal experience and practice and reflect what they hoped to convey to others and what was important to them personally. Their enthusiasm and the freshness with which they approached the teachings was impressive.

What MBSR Means To Me

Settling down and moving into a comfortable position that allows you to quiet and be reflective, ask yourself the questions below:

What do I believe MBSR is about?

_____

_____

_____

What interests me about it?

_____

_____

_____

If I decide to teach it or am teaching it, what is the motivation for that?

_____

_____

_____

As you ask these questions to yourself, you can repeat them and note the thoughts that arise, as well as any sensations that accompany the thoughts. Are you calm, excited, nervous as you reflect on this question? Where is this expressed in your body? How is it felt? What do you learn as you reflect on this question? Jot it down. You can do this more than once as each new moment can lend itself to greater discovery.

I learned:

_____

_____

_____

TEACHING MBSR: CORE COMPETENCIES

I've been involved in MBSR for many years now but I still get nervous before a new cycle of classes. I never know what to expect, either from group members, or myself. The curriculum has become a part of me but how it is conveyed masterfully is dependent on many factors such as the skill of the teacher, the composition of the group and the depth of understanding and skill in group process. This varies over cultures and is not easy to assess or quantify, but after viewing many teachers and classes/groups, six core competencies are essential in assessing excellence and maintaining high standards for teaching MBSR or other Mindfulness-Based courses.

A personal mindfulness practice is essential and underlies each of the competencies. The competencies listed below refer to group programs, but can also be applied to individual work.

CORE COMPETENCIES

1. Coverage, pacing and organization of the material

2. Relational skills

3. Embodiment of mindfulness

4. Guiding mindfulness practices

5. Conveying course themes through interactive teaching

6. Holding of group learning environment

Competence in Teaching Mindfulness-Based Courses: Concepts, Development and Assessment. (Crane, Kuyken, Williams, Hastings, Cooper & Fennell, 2012)

Section 4

SETTING THE FOUNDATION

Program Themes

As you read more about the sequence of classes and their themes, Remember: MBSR is about being rather than doing. There can be a tendency to strive to get it right, meet another person's expectations or have false expectations of how we should be. As I supervise people or coach them in implementing MBSR, I always ask, *"how is it being lived in you? What are you discovering? What is your learning edge?"*

Remember: We are already perfect. The program is designed to help us reconnect to our wholeness.

Remember: Our common humanity. There is no "other," no separation between leader or participant, simply different positions.

Remember: Kindness and compassion. It is OK to make mistakes, simply **S.T.O.P** and give yourself a chance to recover and go on.

Remember: Be authentic, listen and trust your own inner voice. It is also important to note that, though there are separate themes for each class and one builds on another, there is a wholeness to the program. The goal is greater insight into the working of our own mind/body and the effect of our actions. By directly experiencing what is and practicing acknowledging rather than judging, we begin to see the filters through which we view the world and our automatic reactions, which may or may not be serving us.

Remember: The attitudes being cultivated, beginners mind, letting go, letting be, non-striving, trust, acceptance, non-judging and kindness.

Remember: It's about liberation.

Stop
Take a breath
Open, observe
Proceed

WHERE IS YOUR ATTENTION NOW?

What are you experiencing in your body?
What thoughts are you having?
What is the feeling sense? Mood? Pleasant, unpleasant, neutral?
Allow yourself to experience this moment . . . and the next . . . noticing what changes.

49

The MBSR form has not changed much over the years. The themes for the nine sessions (this includes the All-Day Session) build upon each other and have remained constant, but advances in neuroscience have been added. Each class revolves around mindfulness, practicing it formally as well as informally and infusing it into daily life.

Practice in paying attention to ALL that arises in the field of awareness without judgment, in body, mind and feelings with the intention to learn rather than judge is basic throughout, as is acceptance, "letting-be." Practice is tender, sensitive and also disciplined. Inherent to it is compassion and a willingness to acknowledge that being human means we are vulnerable and fallible. Awareness helps us be with rather than resist what we don't like.

THEMES OF MBSR SESSIONS

Orientation - Introduction to the program and assessment of compatibility

Session 1: Foundational, establishes group guidelines, safety, support and beginning of community. Introduces mindfulness experientially with raisin and body scan, and a brief sitting meditation focusing on the breath and a few standing yoga poses.

Session 2: Perception and how it affects responses.

Session 3: Emphasis is on being present in mind and body moment by moment - practice of yoga and meditation.

Session 4: Examination of stress and habitual, automatic reactivity that perpetuates stress and dis-order rather than ease.

Session 5: Coping and the effect of emotional reactivity to health or illness.

Session 6: Communication

Session 7: Integrating mindfulness practice into daily life.

Session 8: Review of practices and on-going support to maintain practice.

Session 1: The First Five Minutes

Below is a transcript of the first five minutes of session one in MBSR that I led at The Center for Mindfulness. My intention was to welcome people, establish a sense of trust and safety and begin to weave in the themes of the course. As you read it, notice the language and key points.

"Welcome. How wonderful to see you . . . I hope you can see this class as an adventure . . . and also find that there's a certain excitement and even wonder in this process of being here . . . experiencing what's here in this moment and being able to observe it with a sense of not knowing but allowing in a way that can teach us what we need to know. Is anyone here because their life is perfect? [Laughter], not me either . . . in fact, as I get older new things appear whether they are in my body or my mind or outside me. It's always something . . . so how do we meet what is here and what can we learn from paying attention in a way that is not judgmental?"

I continue, my voice is hoarse and someone gives me a cough drop.

"Oh what a treat; someone got me a cough drop, so nice. Thank you so much. I guess the other thing to learn is how we are all connected and how inter-dependent we are. How I am affects how you are. How you are affects how I am. And that is how I see the class. This boat of life is a big one and we are all in it. We are all partners in discover . . . how am I living my life now? What can it teach us? . . . What happens here is up to you."

Receiving the cough drop and acknowledging it is a choice point. I could have just said, thank you, and continued my introduction to the class, but it seemed to me a perfect way to demonstrate kindness and inter-connection that arose spontaneously and directly in the classroom.

As I am speaking, some latecomers arrive and are welcomed. I have people turn to each other, say hello, then there is a pause, and I continue.

". . . What happens here, much of it is up to you. It is really your responsibility to show up, to pay attention to what arises and to learn from it the best you can with kindness, generosity, compassion . . . . I like to think of this class as a support, a place of encouragement that is safe and protected."

In reading the above, notice what stood out to you and its intention. If you like, you can circle them and examine their intention.

For example: How Wonderful - Desire to acknowledge participants for making the decision to take the program and create an environment that is positive and recognizes accomplishments. Make people comfortable and provide encouragement and support for them to bring mindfulness into their lives.

Class is an Adventure - Planting the seed for self-discovery and entering into the unknown.

THE GO AROUND

As the class continues, **confidentiality is established and people promise to respect privacy** and not to identify anything of a personal nature from a person in the group. We then go around the room and each person introduces himself and states what brought them to the group. **Permission is given to just say their name and not to talk and pass if they wish.** This can be a time to introduce key concepts or clarify any misconceptions about the class depending on what is being said. It is also a time to connect to others and experience the commonality of stress.

Many realize how their problem is similar to another person's in the group. This decreases isolation and separation as well as creating bonds and enhancing group cohesion. For example, in a first class during the introductory go around one woman, in stating her goals, said that she wanted to be more present with her kids rather than think about what she had to do next. The teacher thanked the woman for sharing and then paused, looked around the room and asked if others could relate to this. Many raised their hands and this served to further connect the discussion on what it means to be present.

Many talk about getting rid of thoughts, or "I want to get off the train" (of thought). When this arises, and it always will, the teacher then has an opportunity to clarify how to work with unwanted thinking (acknowledge the thought free of judgment but then bring your attention back to the present).

GUIDELINES

- No fixing.
- Self-care–listen to your own body for what it needs.
- Be committed and do the home practice but *don't try too hard to relax.*
- Be willing to change and be accepting of impermanence.
- Examine and acknowledge resistance.
- Show up.
- Self-Responsibility - Doing the home practice is important but up to you. Let us know if you have questions or can't attend a session.

KEY ELEMENTS OF SESSION 1

If you were the teacher or facilitator, how would you begin a class? What do you think are the key elements?

_____

_____

_____

If you were a participant in a formal MBSR class, what would you expect? Like to receive?

_____

_____

_____

What would inspire you and gain your active participation in the program?

_____

_____

_____

What is authenticity?

_____

_____

_____

What is the role of self-disclosure?

_____

_____

_____

INTRODUCING MINDFULNESS EXPERIENTIALLY

When I am introducing mindfulness, I do my best to make it as simple and clear as possible. I want it to be invitational and activate curiosity and even wonder. Rather than lecture, I create experiences that can be observed and felt directly in the present moment. An object that is familiar, but can be examined with all the senses, like a raisin, is used. It can be revelatory and sets the stage for further investigation of the "ordinary."

GOALS

- Language is clear and simple
- Activate curiosity and wonder
- Introduce mindfulness experientially through direct experience
- Cultivate beginner's mind
- Investigate familiar objects to foster inquiry and discover assumptions
- Be curious and open to new information
- Connect, establish a relationship to the individual or group you are teaching
- Establish a sense of community and safety

THE RAISIN

Sometimes we don't appreciate the wonder of our aliveness because it is familiar. The breath is an example of this. We often take for granted being breathed - until we get sick and our breathing is compromised or we are exerting ourselves and becoming breathless. The same can be said of objects, nature and even loved ones. The ordinary is truly extraordinary if we bring attention to it and are or become willing to really examine it with all our senses, free of expectations and judgment.

In MBSR, we use a raisin to illustrate this point. This exercise is an excellent introduction to mindfulness. In it, each person is given a raisin with the instruction to imagine that they have never seen one before. They are asked to pretend that they are explorers discovering a new territory or that they have just landed from another planet and are given these objects without knowing what they are. The exercise is done in silence, and the instructor asks that all the senses, including hearing (putting it up to their ear) be utilized. Sense by sense, the instructor asks the group what is being observed.

This is done twice; the first with instruction and very slowly, and the second time without instruction and at the participants' own speed. Discussion of what they observed follows either in pairs, the whole group, or both. People often are surprised by the flavor that is released as they bite into it slowly and realize how quickly they normally eat and how their habit takes away from fully experiencing the food. I always give permission not to do the exercise but when it is completed, I ask how it was experienced.

Goals:

1. Concretizing the use of mindfulness utilizing all the senses
2. Developing openness, curiosity and interest in observing the familiar with a fresh perspective
3. Practice in direct experiencing without expectation or judgment
4. Practice in sense awareness; sight, smell, taste, feel and sound are all encouraged in exploring a familiar object but observing it with fresh eyes, ears, etc.
5. Develops awareness of assumptions, expectations and prior conditioning
6. Sets the stage for developing new patterns of behavior
7. Cultivation of attention and awareness of intention

This awareness exercise can be extended to a discussion of mindful eating and can be given as homework to repeat with a portion of a meal.

INSTRUCTIONS FOR THE RAISIN EXERCISE

Hold this familiar object in your hand

- What does it feel like?

- What do you see?

- Does it make any sound?

- How does it smell?

Upon instruction choose one, put it in your mouth and experience it on your tongue. Noticing where it is placed. How it feels. Any changes in your mouth

Pause - take one bite - experience what happens

Repeat - take a breath between each bite and experience the object's transformation until it is no longer in your mouth

Stop

Do It Again Your "Normal" Way - Choose a second raisin and repeat the practice of putting it in your mouth and eating it

What do you notice?

MBSR is experiential. It is not didactic. It is dependent on a willingness to stop and observe mind, body and heart moment by moment in daily life using all the senses.

THE RAISIN EXERCISE

Select a raisin or another object which is familiar and is able to be examined using each of the five senses. Read the instructions and do this exercise first by yourself and then with a friend or colleague. What do you notice as you do this?

The pause between bites is very important. I usually instruct people to take a breath or two and experience what changes in their mouths as they wait to take another bite.

When the object (raisin) is no longer in their mouths and has been swallowed, we pause again.

Can you be curious about the effect of having done this? What happens when you do it without instruction? What is the learning?

_____

_____

_____

_____

HOMEWORK: MINDFUL EATING

Much physical illness comes from improper eating habits. This week, pay attention to the quality and the quantity of the food you put into your body, and what functions eating is performing for you at this moment. Are you eating to nourish your body and to keep it finely tuned? Are you eating to satisfy cravings for taste sensations, to feel fuller, more complete and more secure? Are you aware of the source of the food you are eating? Does much of it come out of factories? Have the foods you eat been processed? If so, how much? What has been removed? What has been added? Are chemicals in food harmless? Do you pay attention at this level?

Try eating with greater awareness, and somewhat slower than usual. As an experiment, you might try intentionally eating one meal a week in silence with your family just to experience the eating itself. In addition, you might consider not reading or watching TV during meals. It will help you become more sensitive to how you eat. Bring increased awareness to your eating with others.

How will you apply this work to your setting or practice? Be specific. Consider the obstacles and how you will address them. Visualize yourself teaching or practicing with your clients or peers.

S.T.O.P.

Stop
Take a breath
Open, observe
Proceed

BODY SCAN: GROUNDING PRACTICE

Bringing awareness to our body is a powerful exercise in awareness. The body is our foundation. Without it, there would be no thought, no breath and no ability to use our sense organs to experience life. Often there is an aversion to being in our body, especially if we are experiencing pain or discomfort, mental or physical. Paradoxically, the more we are able to be in our body, with the intention to observe and be with the sensation, rather than resist it, the easier it is to cope with whatever is present.

By simply observing and allowing, we are working with ourselves rather than resisting what is beyond our ability to control. The more we can observe what arises with compassion and care, the easier it is to be at home and relaxed with our set of circumstances. For this reason, participants are introduced to the body scan in class, but it is given as a home practice to do daily for the first two classes of the course and alternated with yoga for the third week. People are given a CD or can download a scan that they can listen to at home. The traditional scan is 45 minutes, but this can be shortened and adapted depending on the population served. For example, if it is known that a person is experiencing PTSD or is a victim of sexual abuse or trauma, hands and feet are scanned rather than the whole body, and it is done with eyes open rather than closed.

THE BODY SCAN

To do the body scan it is best to get into a comfortable position either lying down with your arms alongside your body, or sitting in a comfortable chair, preferably a recliner. As with the other meditations, it is important to do this in an environment that is protected and quiet and will support your ability to relax. It can be useful to have a blanket handy should you feel cool as you engage in this meditation. Make sure you will not be interrupted. Carving time to be by yourself and with yourself is important. This is a time for you, to nurture and care for yourself.

You can begin by bringing your awareness to your breath and letting it rest in an area where it is easy to observe its effect on the body. If you like you can rest your hand on your belly, imagine the belly is like a balloon filling with air, rising on the in-breath, and falling, like a balloon deflating on the out-breath. Simply noticing, do not try to change your breath in any way but bring awareness to the motion of breathing. You can note whether the breath is slow or fast, even or irregular. Remember, not to judge what is happening, simply observe.

If it feels comfortable you can let your eyes close and mentally sweep through the body beginning at the feet and moving up through the head. Letting yourself experience the whole body as it is now and noticing if there are any particular areas that are sensitive. If there is any resistance to doing this noting the thoughts that accompany this feeling. Can you describe the sensation? How long does it last? What is its degree of discomfort?

Are there parts of the body you can feel easily and others that are barely discernible? Are you experiencing any sensations you wish would go away? Let yourself be aware of these sensations and do your best to open to your experience whatever they are. When you do this, you can notice when you want to push away or change as well as when you want to linger longer. When your attention wanders, notice and bring it gently but firmly back into your body.

If you like, you can imagine your breath traveling down from its entry point into the body down into your extremities. Beginning on the left side and letting your awareness move down the body into your foot on the left side. If you are short for time, you can do both feet together. However, do not rush this process. The more carefully you can bring awareness into your body part, the more precise will be your attention. Slowly, connect to your feet, beginning with the toes, moving into the heel, the soles of your feet, the arch and top of the foot. When you feel that you have observed it fully you can let the foot (feet) dissolve in your awareness and move into the ankle continuing to bring awareness to any sensation that is present. You might feel warmth or coolness, heaviness or lightness, tingles, pain, sharp or dull, pulsing sensations. It might be itchy or throbbing, soft or rough, tense or relaxed, stiff or flexible., vibrating or prickly or indescribable. See if you can be curious, softening into the sensation exploring its duration and your attitude toward it.

If you are not experiencing any sensation, simply note this. If there is a vivid experience in the body, you can bring your attention to it and then when you are ready you can refocus and return to where you were, softening into and breathing with the sensations that emerge as best you can, bringing compassion and kindness with you as you do this.

Repeat this process throughout your body, first the left side and then the right from the bottom of your feet and up through the top of your head. Remembering, if you like, you can use breath to breathe into any strong sensation. If there is any possibility of sexual trauma it is recommended to bypass the genital area and move from your legs into the hips, the buttocks and the core of your body feeling the pelvis from side to side and back to front. Then moving to the back and the base of the spine. Following the vertebrae up and moving your awareness out into the lower back, middle back, upper back, shoulders, arms, elbow, wrist, and hands. Take your time. When ready you can bring attention into the front of the body. Feeling the abdomen, the chest wall and cavity and its vital organs, then the throat, and neck. Moving into the head beginning with the jaw and moving up through the face, mouth, ears, and nose, eyes, eyebrows and between the eyebrows, the forehead and into the scalp.

Letting yourself rest in the sensations of the moment. You may note the release of tension and worries with the out breath and the bringing of vitality and renewal with the in-breath.

If you like, when you have finished scanning the body you can imagine an opening at the crown of the head through which energy enters, and imagine this energy traveling through the body. Resting in any area that requires some attention and caressing it with the breath. You can reverse this process, imagining energy moving in through the soles of your feet and up through the entire body and exiting and releasing at the crown of the head. You may continue to follow this cycle of breath and of energy moving in and out of the body as long (or short) as you like and when you are ready letting your eyes open, wiggling toes and moving body slowly and carefully to an upright position.

You may do this as many times as you like knowing that each time you do this body scan you are taking an active part in your own wellness …

DISCUSSION: WHAT WAS YOUR EXPERIENCE?

This is a purposeful open-ended question designed to foster insight and elicit a broad response. The participants are encouraged to identify specific sensations, thoughts, and feelings describing where they occurred and to what degree. **The instruction to notice with acceptance and non-judgment leads to a very rich discussion of likes and dislikes, pleasant and unpleasant, and reactivity.** How to observe with more equanimity and to breathe with and soften into, "letting-be" lays the foundation for mindfulness training and practice. It also highlights how non-attentive and judgmental we can be. Often discomfort is experienced in both body and mind. There is often a discussion of pain and the reactivity, associations/thoughts and feelings this evokes. Discovering how much of the body is absent of pain is a major realization. People sometimes go to sleep during the body scan and that is normalized, but how to practice "falling awake" rather than asleep is the focus. It is common to lose attention, but the emphasis is on the ability to return to the body rather than berate oneself for not being present. Compassion and letting-be, acknowledging and allowing the body to be as it is presents as a challenge and an important practice. There is also a recognition of impermanence - noticing changes in the body and mind states.

TIPS

1. Remember to be invitational rather than give directions that are commands.
2. Use gerunds; "ing" words are used as much as possible like noticing, experiencing, feeling, witnessing, letting be, releasing, dissolving, etc. rather than commands.
3. Be invitational – "you may, if you like. . ."
4. Be encouraging and kind.
5. Offer the instruction to practice listening to what you need. . .
6. Remember: this is about awareness; not trying to relax. Acceptance brings relaxation and peace.

WHEN LEADING A BODY SCAN

1. Do it from your own awarenessing of your body rather than a script. Practice doing this out loud or record it so it is comfortable and natural.
2. Give permission to adjust position if needed but to stay with the sensation that is experienced as discomfort or pain for at least a few breaths to see what it is and if it will pass.
3. Be aware of your voice, pacing and rhythm as well as tone.
4. Give permission to open eyes if needed (e.g., experiencing overwhelming thoughts or feelings or fighting drowsiness).
5. Bring kindness and compassion into the scan by your voice and choice of words, (gently, with kindness, soften into, etc.).
6. Always begin by connecting to the person you are instructing and adapting what is needed depending on what you observe from their response(s).

COMMON QUESTIONS AND EXPERIENCES FROM THE BODY SCAN

1. I can't find the time (or how will I find the time?).
2. I fell asleep.
3. I felt pain.
4. I felt "weird" or uncomfortable physical sensations such as restless leg, shaking, chills, trembling, heat (etc.).
5. I got restless.
6. My emotions arose: I hate this, I loved it, it's boring.
7. My mind wandered a lot.
8. I left my body.
9. I saw colors.
10. I went to a beautiful place.
11. I thought of all the things I have to do.
12. I couldn't stop thinking.
13. I got anxious.

INQUIRY: THE ART OF WONDERING

The body scan is an opportunity not only to become more intimate with the body and to befriend it, but also to discover more about the mind/body connection. Some general rules to deepen understanding through inquiry:

- Be curious.
- Wonder.
- Do not rush to answer.
- Observe with awareness free of bias.
- Do not fix.
- Ask questions: what happened? Can you describe it? How long did it last? Has this happened before? Is it familiar? What happened next? What are you experiencing NOW?
- Remember: The intention of a body scan is to help us be present to the body and what it is telling us.
- Remember: Acceptance and not being judgmental.
- Remember: Compassion
- **Remember: To soften into sensations specifically rather than globalizing all as pain.**

ABOUT SLEEP

There can be many reasons for falling asleep rather than falling awake. When a person reports they have fallen asleep while doing a body scan, I always ask if they know when. What was the last thing they heard? When did they wake up? Reinforce the noticing and the waking up and encourage a person to be curious as to how long they can stay awake next time, as well as explore when and where the scan was practiced.

You can also suggest that the person open their eyes or move when they notice they are feeling drowsy. Ask when a person is doing the scan and where. If it is at bedtime and takes place in the bed and under the covers, it is paired with relaxation and sleep and that is what will happen. It is conditioned. Explore where would be a better place and time. It is important to evaluate fatigue level. Maybe sleep is needed. It can be merciful if there is a lot of pain, either emotional or physical.

Sometimes I tell how I used to fall asleep doing my body scan so much that it became a habit, and one day I realized I liked going to sleep. I had begun to expect it. When I renewed my commitment to staying awake, and really made the effort to be awake, I was awake to my experience and it actually became interesting to discover what arose as I went through my body.

FEAR AND ANXIETY

Fear can arise as well as anxiety. You can normalize this and help the person speaking by universalizing the human condition and asking who else in the group experienced this (very rarely are they alone). It also encourages others who had difficulty with the scan to speak up and shows that this is normal. **Naming vulnerabilities** establishes a group norm of honesty free of shame or judgment. It enhances connection and support. Emphasizing the importance of anchoring attention to the present moment rather than the past (past anxiety attacks) or worry about the future (another attack) is important.

Every new moment brings a new possibility for change and heightened awareness of what causes the suffering. Congratulating the participant or oneself for acknowledging their anxiety and encouraging continued practice (We are just beginning.) is useful. This is a good time to introduce the power of conditioning and through inquiry help the participant(s) identify automatic thought patterns and triggers. What were your thoughts? How was it felt in the body? How long did it last? What helped them return to the present moment? Can you bring compassion and kindness to yourself when this happens?

Permission can be given to open the eyes, listen to sound or change positions and return to the scan. If there is a concern about a person, it is always helpful to speak to them individually after class to get more information and perhaps refer them to a therapist. If permission has been given, the facilitator can speak to their therapist to determine if the person suffering can tolerate this practice at this time in their life.

Always congratulate people for the effort they are making in doing the practice and noticing what arises . . . and continuing to practice. Encourage patience and giving themselves the experience of all of the practices for the full eight weeks of sessions. You can let them know that you are available and they can let you know if they have questions.

ADAPTING THE BODY SCAN FOR TRAUMA AND PTSD

If a flashback to a past trauma emerges, be free to tell the person to open their eyes, move, listen to sound or sit up if they are lying down. Speak to them privately later to check in and re-evaluate appropriateness for this type of practice.

If it is known that the person has experienced a trauma, you can shorten the scan and use neutral parts of the body such as arms, hands, feet.

Give permission to keep eyes open or move as well as stop if needed to ground self and discuss grounding techniques like bringing awareness to feet touching ground or other touch points, the feel of the body on a mat or chair, etc.

Pain: Many pain patients come to learn Mindfulness-Based stress reduction. Often this is done after many interventions have failed. The hope is often that their pain will go away rather than they can have an attitudinal change toward it that can ease their suffering. The body scan can rivet their attention to their pain, but it can also help them feel the other parts of the body that are pain free. It is also useful to practice experiencing the specificity of sensation and how it varies rather than globalizing all the sensations experienced into one word, "pain" and all that is associated with it.

My brother is a neuroscientist and for many years he worked in a pain clinic. He told me that it was common to have their patients sing words from the musical *"My Fair Lady"* to the tune of *"The Rain in Spain"*. The words are:

"The stress of pain lies mainly in the brain."

One's attitude and what one thinks about the pain affects the ability to cope with it.

The refrain in the song above is *"I think I got it. I think I got it."*

What is "it"? "What do we get?" is the question. What are the thoughts? What is felt? How much resistance is there and how long has it been occurring? What is the strength of this conditioning, especially negative cognitions?

There is a major difference between chronic pain and acute pain. Both are aversive and it is important to know how long the pain has been experienced, its effect on mind, body and daily living. The instruction to soften into pain, breath with it, and bring awareness to it with compassion often feels counter intuitive.

Experientially, however, it is important to recognize aversion and the effect of resistance in the body and in intensifying suffering. Resisting causes contraction and tightening. This creates more pain and suffering. Practice begins with awareness of conditioned responses to the pain and a willingness to let it be and relax with it and around it - and doing it repeatedly with compassion. **There is no quick fix; patience is required.** It is important to recognize that this requires effort, support and a letting go of the wish things were different than they are.

THE BODY SCAN:
MY EXPERIENCE AND RESPONSE

Bring curiosity to experiencing the body scan and awareness to your responses.

Record the script or listen to a body scan that is already recorded by myself or a person trained in MBSR and practice the body scan as you would if you were taking the class, daily for two weeks. Keep a journal and note what arises.

Do your best to free yourself from expectations and allow your responses without judging them. This process and what you discover about yourself is what's important. It is the beginning of change in reducing stress and will influence how you present and guide people in this practice.

The more you practice, the more you can learn and the more effective you will be in experiencing ease and guiding others if you wish to do so.

It is useful to keep a journal and record when you practice and what is observed.

Practice - date and time:_____

    Experience_____

    Response _____

    _____

Practice - date and time: _____

    Experience_____

    Response_____

    _____

Practice - date and time:_____

    Experience_____

    Response_____

    _____

Practice - date and time: _____

Experience _____

Response _____

_____

Practice - date and time:_____

Experience_____

Response_____

_____

Practice - date and time:_____

Experience_____

Response_____

_____

Practice - date and time:_____

Experience_____

Response_____

_____

REMEMBERING

From the moment a person enters a Mindfulness-Based group, there is an emphasis on bringing loving attention to our awareness and where it resides. Again and again in sessions, and at home, we practice remembering.

- We remember to return to NOW.
- We remember compassion.
- We do our best to remember to be forgiving and not hold on to blame, anger, resentment, worry and other negative states.
- We remember we have choices.
- We remember to S.T.O.P and bring attention to our breath, our body, thoughts and feelings?

How can the present moment be a home of rest and renewal when it can open us up to pain, either physical or emotional that we do not want to feel?

SHORT SITTING MEDITATION WITH AWARENESS OF BREATH

In session 1, we also briefly introduce the sitting meditation as both a formal and an informal practice. Breath is used because it is always with us and, with repeated practice, can be an anchor to the present moment. The ability to S.T.O.P and return to breath during the day, as a time out or as soon as one notices agitation, allows it to become a sanctuary, a time out from the ruminations of a mind lost in fear, worry, anxiety, and regret. Only with repeated practice can it be a signal for calming and quieting so we can freshly bring awareness to experience without being reactive.

The sitting mediation can be introduced simply by having people bring awareness to their bodies, noting the position in the chair, or room if standing, and coming into an erect but dignified position (no slouching) - feet flat on the floor, hands and arms relaxed, head parallel to the ground and shoulders level with each other.

The instruction is to bring attention to the breath, without changing it in any way, feeling the inhalation and the exhalation as it moves the body. People are asked to note where they feel it most vividly, "Is it at the nose, the mouth? Do you feel the belly moving? If you like, you can put your hand on the abdomen and imagine it like a balloon filling with air and expanding as you breathe in and falling, deflating as you breathe out."

You can ask if people can feel the pause between an inhalation and exhalation. Is there a stillness? A space? In that mini moment where are you? Who is the you that is observing? What happens next?

Session 2: Establishing Perspective

We are all creatures of habit. Neuroscience has discovered that what fires together wires together. Repeated thoughts and actions lay down neural networks that become well established and conditioned. With prolonged repetition, they become automatic and below our level of awareness. This is often useful; it allows us to walk, pick up objects, eat, drive, cross the street, and engage in the activities of daily living with ease. It can also blind us and keep us trapped in habits and beliefs that create stress and perpetuate behaviors, big and little, that no longer work for us.

Each time we Stop and remember to be here we can contact that inner space that simply is . . .

WHERE YOU PLACE YOUR ATTENTION MAKES A DIFFERENCE

Have you ever been on your way to a new place and you or your GPS made a mistake and you found yourself in the wrong place and had to "recalculate" and begin again? Then the next time you headed for the same place you automatically took the wrong turn and had to "recalculate" for a second time, or perhaps even a third because it became a habit, an automatic response?

This happens with our thoughts. Just today, a patient of mine told me how tired she was of being fearful. She had an opportunity to go away for the weekend to a lovely place by the ocean and cancelled at the last minute because the friend she was going to ask to join her had not been calling her. Her view of herself, and her life, as alone, unloved and victim, clouds her ability to make a call herself and explore the relationship. Her feeling, based on past abuse, colors her thoughts and feelings and supports her sense of being unlovable. Her sense of inadequacy and fear is the lens through which she views the world. I hear this and I take a breath. It is not enough to ask her for evidence that supports these feelings or to urge her to call her friend and reach out. She is not yet able to do this and has enough self-blame.

So we pause, S.T.O.P, and in the silence my patient touches her sadness and we hold it. We, because I pause with her in the silence that silently holds her. The sadness is marked by a heaviness in the center of her chest and a tightness in her belly. It is recognized, it is felt and putting it in words acknowledges how deep these feelings go. Patience, I think, and we shift focus: Can we look at what would enable you to refocus?

Later we will examine her relationship with her friend and what would move her from a passive stance and sense of being a victim to a more active and potent position but first we pause, recognize the sadness, anger, hurt, and then take time to remember all she has accomplished that she never thought possible. Stopping interrupts the cascade of thoughts and feelings and gives room to a new perspective.

With some people, this can be a leap, a sudden revelation and with others, it happens step by step and with time. What is interesting is how we approach the problem and the willingness to bring attention to it *without judgment.* As homework in the first session of MBSR, we give out a small workbook and in it is a blank sheet with nine dots with the instruction to connect the dots in four straight lines without lifting their pencil from the table (see below). People are asked to work on the exercise at home and bring it back the next week. For some, this exercise is very stressful because they can't do it and get upset; others are able to see the solution immediately, some google the answer or give up. The response to the exercise can be as useful as it illustrates and highlights the different ways we respond to challenges and their effect.

CONNECT THE DOTS IN FOUR STRAIGHT LINES WITHOUT LIFTING YOUR PENCIL FROM THE PAPER.

The answer lies in going outside the box.

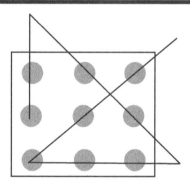

We practice recognizing the boxes that imprison us and perpetuate suffering by taking a step back and observing how we perceive the world. This creates the space, time, and perspective for change.

For example, a man in one of my stress reduction sessions came because he had chronic back pain. He was a roofer and he hated his job, but he was afraid to quit it because it had good insurance. He was diligent in meditating and, as his mind settled and quieted, he stopped thinking so much about how much he hated his job and how trapped he felt. Instead, he focused on coming back to his breath and allowing calm to grow inside himself.

As his mind quieted and he realized he did not want pain to rule his life, it occurred to him that doing the roofing was making the pain worse. This gave him the courage to make plans to quit and find something else for work. Only by stepping back from the problem and giving his mind some rest was he able to go bigger to gain perspective. As space around the problem grew, his perspective shifted and he could leave his box that kept him trapped and make healthier choices.

There is a saying by Confucius: *"The way out is through the door. Why is it that no one will take the exit?"* Each time you catch a repeating thought, a problem, and you release and return to your breath, you are taking the exit.

Stepping Out

Give yourself a specific amount of time to do this exercise, about 5-15 minutes but not more. You can begin by allowing yourself to be comfortable. Give yourself some time to settle into the body and, as you are ready, bring your attention to the breath. Let yourself feel the fullness of the in-breath and the release that comes with the out-breath. As the rhythm of your breathing slows and is even, you can invite your mind to think of a problem that seems to have no acceptable solution.

Using as many senses as possible, bring it and the situation where it is experienced into your awareness as completely as possible. If you like, give the problem a name, note the feelings and what is being felt in your body as you examine it and the thoughts that surround it. If you like, you can write down what you are discovering or even represent it in a drawing. What color(s) would it be, how large, does it have a shape? At the end of your allotted time S.T.O.P.

If you have your eyes closed, you can open them. If you are writing or drawing, put down your pen or art utensils. Mindfully move your arms, your legs, stand or walk. When you are ready, you can return to the breath letting it be your object of attention and examine the problem again.

With kindness and compassion, can you bring space around this problem? In your mind's eye, take an internal step beyond it as if you were a friend who is viewing it from a distance and a fresh perspective.

Can you imagine what it would be like to be outside this box? If you like, you can put your hand over your heart as you do this. Feel the ground under your feet and the body being breathed without effort or force. Note what it feels like to put the box down or aside for now. Perhaps the problem wants to stick and continues returning to your mind. If so, affectionately give it a pat and return your attention to the breath.

Do not expect to solve your problem right now, but bring awareness to your expectations. Imagine they are surrounded by space as is the problem. What is the shape and feel of the problem now? Can you imagine what it would be like to be free of it - letting go of it and being released? How does that feel in the body? The mind? Write it down.

_____

_____

_____

_____

THE SITTING MEDITATION

The sitting meditation is a formal practice that is done in all sessions of MBSR for different lengths of time, beginning with breath as the main object of attention and, mid-way through the sessions, practicing shifting attention - first to breath, then dropping that as primary focus and moving to sensation, sound, feelings of pleasant, unpleasant and neutral. Thoughts can also be an object of attention, catching a thought as it begins and observing its ending and new one beginning. This leads to simply sitting open to all that appears, witnessing it from a solid ground of awareness, present and anchored to the present. This is called choiceless or open awareness. The intention is to directly experience what arises as it arises as free of filtering as possible. It's like being a passenger in a car, seat belt buckled in to watch the scenery as it passes by - and learn about the road and where it leads us.

There are different positions for the sitting meditation. But all emphasize an upright, dignified position that allows the body to be grounded and stable. Pelvis is slightly forward and, if in a chair, feet are flat on the floor. The position is upright, body in alignment and providing a stable foundation that facilitates sustained attention. It is important to be as comfortable as possible, upright but relaxed and not stiff. People are encouraged to listen to their bodies and do what is correct for them, rather than what they *think* is correct or what their neighbor is doing.

If pain is experienced, people are instructed to bring attention to the sensation itself rather than label it as pain, and breath with it, softening into the sensation and only moving if the sensations do not abate and continue causing discomfort.

Sitting Meditation Sample Script

Getting into as comfortable a position as possible, gently closing your eyes and bringing awareness to the experience of breathing . . . See if you can notice the breath as it comes into your body and as it leaves . . . Where do you feel the breath most vividly? Is it at the nostrils, the chest, the belly? . . .

If you like, you can let your hand rest on your belly and feel it rising and falling as you breathe in and out. There's nothing you have to do. Don't try to change it or have it be any particular way . . . allowing, acknowledging and noting what arises . . . witnessing and letting what arises pass without trying to change anything . . . imagining that the mind is like the sky, vast and spacious through which clouds come and go . . ..

When your mind wanders, and it will (this is normal), gently but firmly return your attention to your breath and the motion of breathing . . . If you're having any particularly strong sensation or experience that captures your attention, you can bring your awareness to it and its different sensations, even breathing with, leaning into it gently and with compassion giving it space and holding it in awareness . . . When you're ready, you can return to your breath as the main focus of attention. You can always open your eyes, look around, and then return to your breathing, closing your eyes again when you are ready . . . if judgment arises, noting it and letting it pass, new breath, new moment . . . Remembering kindness . . . leaning into any perceived difficulty. Each time you note your attention has moved away from breath, wonderful, you are strengthening the mindfulness muscle . . . and now you can return to this moment.

NEW BREATH . . . NEW MOMENT . . .

If you like, you can expand your awareness to include sensation, the touch of your body on the chair or other object that is supporting you, the placement of your hands, the weight of your head . . . and any other sensation that appears but letting breath be your primary object of attention. When there is sound, note hearing and sound. When you are aware of thinking you can name the thought, planning, worry, judgment, or the emotion, anger, sadness, fear and observe its effect in the body and return to feeling the breath.

And as you are ready, letting your eyes open if they have been closed, and returning your attention to here . . . congratulating yourself if you like, for taking this time for yourself and your effort in awarenessing.

It is best to do this exercise for a set period, preferably at the same time each day. It is helpful to set the time in advance and do this meditation in a quiet place that is free of interruptions and where you feel safe.

You can tune in to your breathing any time. It can be an anchor to the present moment.

ALTERNATE BREATH AWARENESS

Sometimes just helping a person connect with the breathing process can be an incredibly relaxing and helpful process, but for others, it can bring up anxiety, fear or pain. For this reason, it is important to give choices, such as giving permission to open eyes, feel your feet on the ground, focus on sound (which, being objects outside of the self, can be reassuring and grounding). When doing this exercise with people who may be on medication or cognitively impaired, it is helpful be alongside them guiding them. It can be paired with words of reassurance and calming like, "Breathing in . . . health and vitality, or a sense of well-being . . . and noticing that you are here (alive) now . . . Breathing out . . . releasing toxins, worries, etc.

Always pausing, bringing awareness yourself to the movement of the person's breath, pausing and talking/listening to their responses if that seems needed. If you are working with a person who is cognitively impaired, follow their train of associations. Your being with them and a gentle touch may be all that is needed.

LENGTH OF TIME

In MBSR, awareness of breathing as a focus of attention and as an anchor to the present moment is introduced briefly for 1-2 minutes in the orientation and the first session. As the sessions progress, the time increases and becomes 20, then 30 minutes. At home, the CD (which will be given out in session 5) moves from the breath to include the body, sensations, sounds, emotions and feelings and thoughts. These are introduced separately and are paced so that there are long pauses in between each one. The meditation ends with choiceless awareness, which is also called bare attention and means that the mind rests on whatever comes into awareness. This is an advanced practice and requires the ability for sustained and relaxed awarenessing.

Personal Practice: Sitting Meditation

Find a place where you can sit quietly and undisturbed by interruptions. Decide in advance the period of time you will be sitting, where you will do this and when. If you live with others, it is recommended that you explain to members of your household what you are doing and why. It is recommended that you choose a time that works for all so there will be cooperation and understanding. This may require some negotiation and is itself a part of the practice as is your willingness to make time in your day to do this.

It can be helpful to create a meditation journal, writing down when you meditated, how long, and notes about the experience. Do this as a scientist might with the intention to learn and not to be judgmental.

Date_____ Beginning Time_____ Ending Time_____

Experience:

Date_____ Beginning Time_____ Ending Time_____

Experience:

Date_____ Beginning Time_____ Ending Time_____

Experience:

Date_____ Beginning Time_____ Ending Time_____

Experience:

Date_____ Beginning Time_____ Ending Time_____

Experience:

Date_____ Beginning Time_____ Ending Time_____

Experience:

Section 5

MINDFUL MOVEMENT

Session 3: Yoga and Mindful Movement

I always think of this session as a mini-retreat as the emphasis is on practice. It often begins with some standing yoga, which can be referred to as stretches, and a guided sitting meditation. I also like to ask about home practice. People have been asked to do the body scan daily for two weeks. This means they have hopefully changed their daily schedule to give themselves the time and privacy to do the scan and are more able to be in their bodies.

The body scan starts with the toes on purpose, because, as James Joyce noted in *The Dubliners*, *"Mr. Duffy lived a short distance from his body."* Sadly, many of us are like Mr. Duffy, believing that awareness is a mental activity alone and primarily located in the head. We ignore our bodies until something goes wrong.

Yoga is a Sanskrit word and is a yoking of mind and body, unifying and harmonizing the two. Yoga and meditation complement each other and yoga is an integral part of MBSR. The two are doorways that open into a unity and wholeness that lead to insight and wisdom. The yoga in MBSR is not to become physically fit. It is about flexibility and resilience. It brings awareness into the body and reminds us to live in the body as well as the mind. In discussing home practice, the theoretical (why we do the body scan) meets the practical. What are people noticing and how do they respond to what is being witnessed and felt? Has their perception changed and if so how?

The following yoga (stretches) are from the MBSR program at the University of Massachusetts Medical School. They can be adapted to being done in a chair or a bed. If a person cannot do either, they can also be visualized. Non-striving and listening to the body to tell you how long to hold a pose or how far to go in any of the positions is emphasized.

The stretches begin with a resting pose, because the body is fully supported by the ground allowing for deep relaxation with the legs spread apart about six inches, arms alongside body, palms facing the ceiling. If a person has back problems, they are instructed to bring their feet toward their buttocks and have knees pointing up toward the ceiling.

BEGINNING INSTRUCTIONS

Invite a person to lie on their back, if there is room and you are able. When the room is small, we often recommend the astronaut position, bringing the body close to a chair and resting the lower legs on the seat of a chair.

If a person prefers to sit in a chair and do chair yoga that is also fine, as is not doing them and visualizing the positions.

The resting position is repeated between poses and is as important as the ability to lift a leg or rotate the pelvis. The focus of attention is body - and breath. Below is a list of some poses used at the Center for Mindfulness. Participants are instructed to listen to the recording of these poses along with a guided meditation that they have been given and follow its instructions every other day. It is recommended *that they check with their doctor or physical therapist if there are any questions about safety.*

Lying Down Poses

- Resting - Supine Pose
- Full Body Stretch
- Pelvic Rock and Tilt
- Rocking and Rolling Back-n-Forth
- Knees to Chest
- Cat Pose
- Cow Pose
- Bird Dog (both sides)
- Bridge Pose
- Supine Twist (both sides)
- Leg Stretch (both sides)
- Prone Leg Stretch (both sides, resting on the front)
- Modified Cobra
- Resting - Supine Pose

Standing Poses

- Arm Reach
- Stretching – Picking Grapes
- Leg Lifts – front, side, back
- Pelvic Circling
- Head, Neck, Shoulder Stretches

CHAIR YOGA

Head and Neck:

Turn the head from side to side, looking over the shoulder. Look up and look down and

Shoulders:

Roll shoulders forward and backward. Rolling shoulders forward toward each other on out-breath and circling them down and back toward each other on in-breath. Repeat – slowly and mindfully.

Arm Lift:

As you breathe in, raise arms out and to the sides palms facing outward and then up and overhead, palms facing each other and stretching up to feel the stretch in your whole upper body. Stay there for a few breaths and then stretch up high on one side and then the other bringing the arms down on the out-breath and bringing awareness to the sensations as they come to rest alongside the body.

Knees:

Lift knees, one at a time.

Legs:

Extend calves and feet, one at a time, rolling feet in and then out.

Standing or sitting, become aware of the floor under your feet.

Move slowly and mindfully in any way that feels good to you!

Back and Forward Bends:

Sitting on the chair so your feet are placed flat on the ground, slowly raising the arms overhead as you breathe in and lifting the arms slightly backwards, opening the chest and on the out-breath slowly coming forward, leading with the arms as much as is comfortable, letting the hands go towards the floor or, if possible, resting on it for a few breaths releasing into it and then coming up slowly.

Spinal Twists:

Breathing in, straighten up your spine in the chair. As you slowly exhale, begin to twist around to the right, starting with your hips, then ribs, Place your left hand on your right knee or thigh. Twist your shoulders and place your right hand on the chair or arm of the chair. Finally, turn your neck and head to look behind you. Take a few breaths and, with each in-breath, lift up through the crown of your head, and with each out-breath twist a little more continuing to lengthen your spine if possible. Then slowly unwind the twist, and come back to center on the exhalation.

Repeat for 3 to 5 breaths on the other side.

Make sure your exhalation is at least as long as your inhalation.

TIPS FOR YOGA

Practice the positions yourself maintaining awareness in the body.

Pay attention to the act of moving into a posture and the sensation of being in it, as well as returning to a resting position.

If you are going to lead another in mindful movement or the above stretches, practice saying the words and giving instructions as you do the pose or movement.

Remember to advise people to take care of themselves and listen to their bodies.

Remember to remind people that this is not about striving or pushing to do a pose, but is a deep listening to the body. Its purpose is to enhance flexibility, awareness and resilience. It is about befriending the body and discovering its limits and **not** pushing beyond them.

HOMEWORK AFTER WEEK 3

Alternate body scan with yoga. Ask yourself every day: What is my body needing right now? Am I allowing some aspect of my body or mind to be in an unhealthy condition through neglect, inattention, or inactivity? What am I doing today to care for myself?

EVENT DIARY

In week two, participants recorded pleasant events. This is followed in week three by a daily record of unpleasant events - to name the stressor (the unpleasant event) noting its trigger and the thoughts, emotions and sensations that are present. (See diary sheets on pages 87 & 88)

SUMMATION OF CLASSES 1-3

I view the first three sessions of an MBSR class as foundational. During this period, mindfulness is introduced and the body scan has been practiced for two full weeks and part of a third. A short sitting meditation with awareness of the breath and mindful movement (yoga), standing and lying down are introduced. Much of classroom discussion is focused on practicing mindfulness and clarifying understanding. Motivating participants to take time for themselves not only by taking 45-60 minutes to listen to and follow guided meditations but to being more awake and aware in daily life is a priority. Connections begin to be made between difficulties in practice and habitual patterns of thought and behavior that are not constructive. Compassion, kindness and the importance of self-care are emphasized along with being non-judgmental.

S.T.O.P.

Stop
Take a breath
Open, observe
Proceed

Evaluating Practice

How are you now understanding mindfulness?

_____

_____

What is your formal practice? How long, how often?

Body Scan _____

Sitting Meditation _____

Yoga _____

Walking _____

What helps you in taking the time and creating the space for practice?

_____

_____

What is its effect?

_____

_____

Is it making a difference in your life? If so, how?

_____

_____

Informally: How are you incorporating mindfulness throughout the day?

_____

_____

What helps you remember to pause and live in the present?

_____

_____

WALKING MEDITATION

This can be both a formal and informal practice. Thich Nhat Hahn, founder of Plum Village, Zen Master, global spiritual leader, poet and peace activist, talks about kissing the earth when you walk. For many people, when the mind is agitated, it can be calming to walk and have attention focused on the feet and the act of taking a step, lifting, moving, placing, shifting weight, rebalancing and taking another step. Attention is on the feet and the connection with the ground. To refine attention, a person can be instructed to lift on the inhale and place the foot on the exhale.

*"Every path, every street in the world is your
walking meditation path."*

— Thich Nhat Hanh

Section 6

EXAMINING STRESS AND
COPING STRATEGIES
REACTING VS. RESPONDING

The Effect of Feelings: Pleasant, Unpleasant and Neutral

The second foundation of mindfulness is awareness of feelings. This can include emotions, but it refers to bringing awareness to feeling tones, the experiencing of pleasant, unpleasant or what lies between these states, which is sometimes labelled neutral. These feeling tones can influence how we respond to events, mental and physical, inside us, or outside ourselves. We are hard wired to protect ourselves, and **by resisting what we consider to be unpleasant and craving or clinging to what we perceive as pleasant, we perpetuate suffering**. Often this is unconscious. Bringing awareness to these feelings and resulting thoughts and sensations opens the door to change - and greater happiness.

For example, I was recently introducing mindfulness to a group of elders in an assisted living facility. Some had come to the room with walkers; a few were in wheel chairs or walked with a cane. They had come together to discuss wise aging led by a social worker and a clergyman. For most, the assisted living facility represented the last stage of their lives and a loss of independence. Their minds were alive, but the aging process had altered both body and mind.

I invited them to pause and bring attention to the position of their body and the feel of breath moving in and out of the body with curiosity and kindness. The leaders then asked the group how they felt about aging and living in the facility. Many of the thoughts and words they used to describe this were negative.

> One woman was particularly distressed. *"I've lost 'me,'* she said.
> She had been a writer, *"My mind isn't working like it used to. I can't write anymore . . .
>   There's nothing to do here. "I can't grow anymore."*
> Others in the group shifted in their chairs, uncomfortable.
> One woman spoke to her. *"You can write and there's a lot to do here."*
>   *"No one gives me a chance to mourn."* The first woman responded. The room was quiet
> and the clergyman asked the rest of the group, *"How do you feel?" "Angry,"* said one, *"loss,"*
> said another, *"frustrated, sad,"* said a third.

As this was happening, I felt my eyes tearing, a constriction in my throat and an awareness of sadness. Then thoughts followed. The first thought was how I really did not want to go to an assisted living facility to live or to be infirm. I recognized "fear" and named it to myself. The feeling tone was "unpleasant." Then I began mentally thinking about inquiry.

The question "how do you feel?" seemed very non-specific to me. I wondered where in the body were there sensations. I also noted that the facilitator had not asked the woman speaking more about how she felt but moved to the whole group. Judgment: I thought it would be more skillful to stay with the woman longer and inquire into her statement about needing to mourn and feeling she was not allowed to do this. As this thought entered my awareness and I began mentally evaluating what a skillful inquiry might be, there was a shift. The feeing tone of unpleasant was much milder. Sensation shifted to my belly. It was tighter, a sign of discomfort, uneasiness and a recognition that it was hard for me not to be the leader and respond to this woman as I might in an MBSR class. As my thoughts shifted to my pre-frontal cortex, and I began problem-solving, I was absorbed in thought and there was less body awareness. The feeing tone was in the neutral range.

There was no good or bad, right or wrong to my responses but awareness allowed movement of feelings, thoughts and sensations. I didn't feel stuck or lost in any particular state. How might the woman who lost "me" be met so she could adapt to change? What allows us to take a step back so there is no me to be lost but a being to be found?

The diaries below are designed to help us take that step back and observe the sequence of events, thoughts, sensations and feelings to discover our habitual responses and examine their effects. As you fill out the journal and bring into awareness reactions to events that are felt as pleasant or unpleasant remember not to be judgmental or self-critical.

What arises is conditioned. We feel what we feel and think what we think. It's part of being human, but we don't need to drown in these thoughts and feelings or get stuck there. If you catch yourself doing this, pause, congratulate yourself for noticing this habit and return to the here and now. Remember, it's a process of discovery. With awareness, there is choice. Without it, the same patterns blindly get repeated. "You get what you get but don't get upset" is a slogan now taught to children in schools. We will get upset, it's inevitable, but we don't need to stay there - next moment, new opportunity.

PLEASANT EVENTS DIARY

Each day, be as specific as you can in describing an experience that is pleasant and noting what you experienced in mind and body as well as what happened next.

	Sunday	Monday	Tuesday	Wednesday	Thursday	Friday	Saturday
Triggering Event							
Thoughts							
Feeling Tone							
Emotions							
Sensations							
Outcome							

What are you learning by doing this?

_____

UNPLEASANT EVENTS DIARY

Be as specific as you can in describing an experience that is unpleasant and noting what you experienced in mind and body, as well as what happened next.

	Sunday	Monday	Tuesday	Wednesday	Thursday	Friday	Saturday
Triggering Event							
Feeling							
Thoughts							
Emotions							
Sensations							
Consequences							

Review your diaries and your relationship to the events considered either pleasant and unpleasant. How did the perceptions and sensations differ? What was similar? What can you learn from this?

Sessions 4 and 5: Stress and Coping Strategies

We are now in the heart of this eight-week course in MBSR, and it is a time that many are discovering what is wrong with them rather than what is right. Doubt arises, and it takes effort, patience and trust to keep practicing as well as maintaining the other attitudes discussed earlier.

Judgment can arise and be vicious; acceptance is not easy nor is letting-go or not striving for change. Attentional stability and flexibility are more established but it still can be very challenging to examine the automatic reactions and conditioning that perpetuate stress.

At this juncture, it is common for people to be impatient for their symptoms and problems to disappear. Unpleasant feelings may predominate as the expectation that there should be no more pain, emotional or physical, is not met. Awareness heightens sensitivity rather than lessening it.

Answering the question, "why keep practicing," or defending mindfulness is a trap. Instead, it's useful to refer to the pleasant and unpleasant event diaries and support the investigation of habitual reactions to each.

Rather than try to make a person feel better or fix the problem it is much wiser to compassionately (and non-judgmentally) get more information about the problem. This sometimes requires a leap of faith. This is especially true when a person is new to practice and may be very averse to sitting quietly and being an observer of mind, body, thoughts and feelings free of judgment and reactivity. The weekly journal diary of pleasant and unpleasant events helps.

WHY PRACTICE MINDFULNESS?

$\underline{S}$top

$\underline{T}$ake a breath

$\underline{O}$pen, observe

$\underline{P}$roceed

Can you bring compassion and kindness to yourself and continue being aware of your automatic reactions to pleasant and unpleasant events? What is helpful to you in maintaining your commitment to mindfulness and practicing it daily formally and informally?

_____

_____

_____

GOALS IN SESSIONS 4 AND 5

- Understand stress and what creates it.
- Examine the effect of feelings, pleasant, unpleasant and neutral.
- Bring awareness to causality - the interplay of thoughts, feelings and sensations.
- Practice tender acceptance and kindness.
- Use awareness to regulate our automatic reactions.
- Learn about our conditioning and pattern of response.
- Realize we have choices.
- Continue practicing mindfulness and apply it throughout the day.

An example from Session 4 that highlights the difficulty of examining stress and meeting it with openness and equanimity:

I like to begin classes with some stretches to help people settle and enter into the session with freshness. This helps them let go of thoughts and feelings from earlier in the day. I also have a check-in to clarify any questions regarding the home practice and to see how people are doing. Below is an example from a fourth session. I was asking about the sitting meditation that had been practiced in class and at home.

The first response I got regarding my inquiry was from a woman who often monopolized airtime and spoke in a tone of voice that I perceived as whiny and pitched in a way that I found negative and challenging.

"Are we supposed to set a timer?" she asked.

"What did you do?" I replied, not wanting to answer the question for her.

She responded, *"If I had the time, I did it, but this week was crisis management week. If I had a moment to do it (sit and bring attention to her breath) I just sat and did it and when it was done, it was done, but I had no idea how long it was . . . I'm sure it was not 10 minutes."*

As she said the last part, the tone of her voice changed.

I noted the vocal shift and asked what that represented. Internally I thought this could be a moment of insight. I wondered whether she was judging herself or worrying about what was "right" and thinking it was not sufficient? Perhaps this was a pattern of hers and she could recognize it and examine its effect on her.

The woman, ignoring my question, asked again if she should set a timer. Deciding that it would not be fruitful to push her to respond I answered her and said yes, it was helpful to decide in advance how long to practice. I also congratulated her on doing a meditation even though she had been busy.

"How wonderful you paused throughout the day and did what you could. What happened next?" I asked. *"Did you notice any difference in how you approached your work?"*

"I just went on," she replied, not directly answering my question or engaging in reflection.

I felt my body contract during this exchange remembering that I've not known how to meet this woman. She often was the first person to speak or to ask a question or make a statement. I found it hard to connect to her and use our dialogue in a way that was constructive not only to her but also to the other class members. She also took up a lot of airtime. There was a choice now for me as teacher - do I attempt to have her investigate what she labelled as crisis week and her responses or not? I was aware of my irritation and desire to move on and hear from other group members but since the topic for the week was stress and questioning her further could be helpful I decided to continue.

"What helped you during the week?" I asked.

"I didn't have time to do anything else. That was all I did," she said, somewhat defensively, *"except for Friday when I had a little time to do a full body scan, which I've enjoyed expecting it would help me relax and it set me into a panic attack (everyone laughed). I just had to turn you off and go to sleep."*

I laughed and it was genuine. She was funny. Hoping I could join with her and we could have a deeper discussion, my irritation evaporating for the moment, I spontaneously responded,

"I have to tell you I just love the way you say this" (still smiling and laughing a little).

She went on, *"Through the whole thing I'd say will you shut up? (She did the whole scan). You'd talk about the ankle and I'd say, "Will you shut up? I don't care about my ankle, I'm having a panic attack, I don't care about my calf. Will you shut up? I just had to turn you off and go to sleep."*

I then asked, *"Did it help?"* Is there anything you learned about that process? What did you learn?"

"I took control and I turned you off." She then paused to see my reaction.

Keeping my voice even and staying calm, I validated that taking control is important and is needed in managing stress. I then asked if she could bring attention to the resistance itself and have that be a means of control, too? Was turning off the CD the only way to have control? How about changing one's attitude?

I was aware that this could be an opportunity to examine the relationship of attitude to outcome. I knew I could have asked whether her reaction to the scan and to the work she had to do was a familiar pattern. Was it her habit to force herself to do what she thought she should do but resent it? Could she see its connection to her fatigue and exhaustion and how her resistance perpetuated her suffering?

I did not feel there was an openness to insight and did not want to confront her or have her take up more class time. I also did not want to get into a struggle with her and get stuck in a reactivity myself, so I decided it would be more fruitful to move on. As I had this thought, another person in the group spoke and asserted the need to go into the body and feel sensations when there is a sense of disturbance.

"I am a manager and sometimes have to fire people," he said. *"I anticipate being stressed when I have to do this so I take a few breaths to calm myself before I talk to the person. Then I am with him rather than my symptoms and anxiety."*

Knowing himself and the situations that caused him stress was skillful. He listened to his body and felt his heart beating more rapidly and his respiration increasing as he thought about the upcoming firing. This was the signal that told him to calm and prepare himself for the interview so he could be fully present with his employee.

Another person began to describe how she used the S.T.O.P. prior to a tennis match with a new partner. Discussion then ensued about acknowledging stressful situations and how the body was our early warning system. Usually there was an unpleasant feeling which activated thoughts of fear and anxiety. Recognizing this and using the S.T.O.P interrupted these thoughts and sensations. Then it was possible to proceed.

Another person experienced back pain. She described that she was trying to "soften into it - sensation by sensation - and was catching some of her thoughts about her condition and practicing interrupting the thought and coming back to now, this moment, and refocusing on her direct experience. Sometimes it was her position in the chair, other times she opened her eyes or felt her feet on the ground. Then she could return and lean into the pain and not fight it.

"I'm realizing I am not my pain. It's not who I am, and it doesn't have to rule my life. It still hurts but I'm going out a bit more and I met a friend last week for coffee."

CHALLENGES

- Acknowledging our patterns of defense without being reactive
- Recognizing the effect of aversion and resistance
- Leaning into and exploring discomfort
- Observing the effect of thoughts and feelings in creating and perpetuating stress like anxiety and panic
- Practicing acceptance.
- Practicing patience and trust, kindness and compassion
- Taking a chance to do something different; entering into the unknown
- Maintaining a commitment to bringing awareness to ALL our experience
- Being in the present moment
- Repetition and practice - returning again and again to this moment without being self-critical and judgmental
- Knowing change is possible and is in fact happening as you read this
- Learning what we do have control over: Our attitude
- Acknowledging our humanness and vulnerability
- Being able to receive support.
- You don't have to like what is happening, but you need not put up resistance in vain.

Know when too much is too much; it is skillful to S.T.O.P. rest, renew and refocus.

INSPIRATIONAL SAYINGS

> *"You can't stop the birds of suffering from flying over your head but you **can stop** them from nesting in your hair."*
> — Chinese proverb

> *"The one thing that cannot be taken from man is his ability to choose his attitude in any given set of circumstances."*
> — Viktor Frankl, holocaust survivor, *Man's Search for Meaning*

I say to myself, *"Yes to life and all that is in it."*

Every day I appreciate being here - alive! And practice gratitude.

STRESS: A PSYCHOLOGICAL DEFINITION

The research psychologists, Richard Lazarus and Ruth Folkman, see stress as transactional and interactive and dependent on the relationship between the person and the environment that is *appraised* by the person as taxing or exceeding his or her resources and endangering his or her wellbeing. Lazarus states that stress is experienced when a person perceives that the "*demands exceed the personal and social resources the individual is able to mobilize.*"

How we interpret an event is more important than the event itself.

KEY WORDS

- Demand
- Perceive
- Appraise
- Relationship

STRESS REACTION - AN AUTOMATIC PHYSIOLOGICAL RESPONSE AFFECTING EVERY SYSTEM IN THE BODY

This is a primal reaction and involves the more primitive part of the brain, which acts so quickly that our thinking brain, the pre-frontal cortex, cannot respond. This protects us from threat, causing hormones, such as adrenaline and cortisol, to surge through the body and directing blood into the periphery, our arms and legs, to prepare us for flight or fight. This response is normal and needed to survive. Once the threat is over, we return to our initial state of balance and homeostasis, but if we continue to feel threatened, anxious and worried, as happens with post-traumatic stress, panic, and anxiety, we are in a perpetual state of stress and don't recover.

The body likes to be in a state of homeostasis so it adapts to chronic stress but this impacts the system over time. For example, if you break a leg and use crutches or have hip surgery, you rely on other parts of the body for movement and after a while, your good leg or hip begins to hurt.

Chronic stress can result in fatigue, lowered immune system function, aches, pains, asthma, palpitations, gastro-intestinal problems, depression, anxiety and more.

Mindfulness acts as an early warning system to help us know when we are either physically or mentally contributing to a state that over time will create problems. Gary Schwartz and Shauna Shapiro describe a model of self-regulation based on mindfulness.

Dis-attention > Dis-connection > Dis-regulation > Dis-order > Dis-ease

But with intention

Attention > Connection > Regulation > Order > Ease

For example, if we are tired or hungry and ignore or push through it, there are consequences. Our concentration can lag, we can get irritable, headaches etc. The same is true of negative mind states. By noting what is arising, paying attention to the messages the body is sending us we can stop, evaluate what is needed and then proceed in a calmer more effective manner. If we ignore our body or don't notice how our thoughts are affecting us, we become disregulated. This state can be so familiar and its stress so prevalent, it is not even noticed until something goes wrong.

THE MIND/BODY CONNECTION

> Can you draw or find an image that represents stress for you?

What gets me going? What are my triggers? A thought? A smell, a feeling?
A particular situation?

_____

_____

_____

What do I experience as threatening and overwhelming?

_____

_____

_____

What do you fear changing or losing - in the future?

_____

_____

_____

What stressors, worries or fears are from past experiences or anticipation of something that might happen in the future?

_____

_____

_____

What is your current experience of stress?

      Stressor

      Thought

      Feeling

      Sensation

Name the stressor and mark where it is experienced in the body

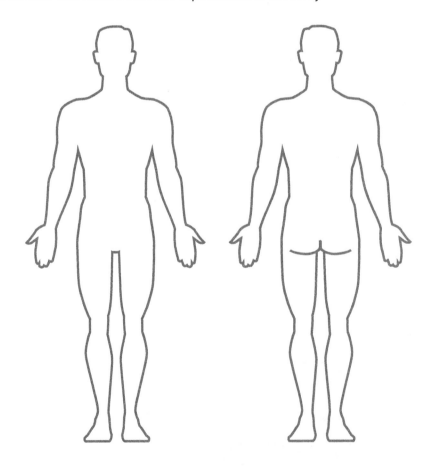

Choose one stressor and allow yourself to bring attention to it, noting when it occurs and where you feel it in the body. Note what triggers it, its duration and frequency and consequences.

Write it down or represent it with an image.

THE STRESS RESPONSE

The word response is used when are actions are not automatic but thoughtful and considered. This happens when we stop and put some space between the stressor and our reaction to it and what we do next. Pausing allows us to begin to think again and access our resources. We can problem-solve, regain our footing and re-center, calm ourselves and cope better emotionally. Frankl wrote, "*In that space is our power to choose our response. In our response lies our growth and our freedom.*"

How one responds is connected to our intention and our values. Everyone is subject to illness, aging, loss and death, but each of us have our own ways of responding and unique trigger points. Mindfulness brings awareness to these triggers and automatic patterns, but it is intention that provides the fuel that creates change and allows us to respond wisely.

Mindfulness-Based stress reduction doesn't tell anyone what to do, but it helps a person bring attention to what and how they think, feel and do and note its effect. From the very beginning, the **response ability** for change lies within each person.

Questions to Consider to Live Fully:

- What is important to me?
- What are my values?
- How congruent are my beliefs and the way I am living?
- What are the effects of my actions, my thoughts, feelings and beliefs?
- Am I living in a way that is ethical, mindful and wholesome?
- Am I either knowingly or unknowingly doing harm to others or to the self?

This, of course, changes day by day and kindness, compassion, patience, and being mindful helps us experience peace and let in joy, even in the face of serious illness. It helps us bring awareness to what is here now to be grateful for and appreciate what is available to us - life itself: A smile, a touch, nature, relationships, a brain that can think, a sip of water or the ability to use a sense organ, hear, see, feel, being awake and alive.

Often these are things that we take for granted unless something goes wrong. The mind tends to note what is pleasant, which we wish would never cease, and what is unpleasant, but what about neutral?

Every day, especially if I am feeling a little bored or restless I note it, take a breath and **remember** to appreciate the normalcy, non-eventfulness of the moment. The car is working. We have flush toilets. My relationships . . . and I pause and am thankful there is no crisis. Sun rises and sets. I am awake.

POINTS TO CONSIDER

1. We are all connected and inter-dependent.

2. How we relate to each other and the circumstances of our lives, including pain, makes a difference.

3. Expectations can cause suffering.

4. Every moment is a precious moment. It means we are alive.

5. Resisting what is being experienced perpetuates misery.

6. Feelings affect perception and the sequence of events that follow.

7. Acceptance and leaning into what is difficult or painful is difficult but is freeing.

8. Change happens.

9. Support, kindness and compassion are important.

10. We can choose our attitude - and it makes a difference.

Letting Be With Guided Meditation and Awarenessing

You can read the meditation below aloud and record it or read it to yourself to become familiar with it. The questions that follow are guides to enhance your awareness. You can journal and write down what you observed or simply note it mentally.

In doing the meditation choose a time and place where and when you will not be interrupted.

Guided Meditation: Letting-Be

You can begin by getting into a comfortable position but one that is upright, dignified and erect. Allow yourself to bring awareness into the position of your body, the feeling of your arms resting on your legs or alongside your body, the connection of your feet to the ground and when you are ready letting your attention rest with the breath. Experiencing the movement of breath, following the inhalation, feeling the length of the exhalation and softening into whatever arises, be it thought, sensation, feeling, expected or unexpected. Letting be - with the body receiving breath and sound - and not attempting to change what is here. Breath by breath, letting be, letting in love, letting in appreciation for the ability to be here feeling the aliveness of body and mind and the exchange between the two.

If you like, you can use a word or phrase for calming - calm, here, alive, peace. Whatever enters your awareness that is comfortable to repeat to yourself again and again. As your breath moves in and out. As you feel change. As the mind produces thought and you can comfortably observe the movement of mind like a vast sky, blue and clear. Observing the weather, clouds coming in and moving through.

You can tenderly feel the effect of a thought or sensation that is experienced as pleasant . . . and tenderly touch what feels unpleasant. Do your best to be awake to what is not felt as either. Note what arises that can be challenging, note what arises that is calming . . . letting be. Allowing each breath, each moment, to be full and complete in itself and the next, entering into it freshly, anew with curiosity and perhaps wonder.

Thoughts will come, thoughts will go. You will notice sensations and sounds. If a stuckness happens, a thought repeats itself again and again, a sensation is painful to lean into, caress it with awareness. Let the hand or arm touch the area in the body that is hurting . . . you can always open your eyes and then close them again as you return to here, this moment, this breath, this body. And you can repeat to yourself a word you have chosen as a gentle reminder to soften, relax and be here, fully as you are, whole, and beautiful in your aliveness and being.

Breath by breath, letting be, letting pleasant be received, letting unpleasant be felt letting it flow through, in and out, up and down, zig zagging, a miracle of aliveness, neurons connecting, wiring and rewiring . . . and letting peace grow because there is no agenda except to be here and rest in the moment. Bringing kindness to the self that is here and opening into the expansiveness of sky and breath moving and changing but always present. Being perfect as you are no matter what the thought, feeling or sensation. Letting experiences come and go. If you find restlessness arriving, boredom, doubt, fear or anger do your best to welcome it, learn from it and notice what changes. Let it go but do not force it, resting in the moment, feeling your body being supported, your feet touching ground, coming into balance again and again. And when you are ready, you can open your eyes if they are closed and change your position viewing world with eyes, heart and mind anew. Peace. Peace. Peace.

Awarenessing The Meditation

Curiosity - What arose in your awareness? Can you name the thoughts, feelings and sensations that were experienced?

_____

_____

Opening-leaning into-breathing with - relaxing into difficulty

If anything uncomfortable and unpleasant arose were you able to explore it with kindness and not be reactive? How did that feel?

_____

_____

Could you ground the experience in the body?

_____

_____

What did you feel?

_____

_____

Where did you feel it?

_____

_____

Could you ground experience in the present moment?

_____

_____

What was the experience? When did it occur?

_____

_____

How long did it last?

_____

_____

How familiar is it? Can you name other times you experienced this?

_____

_____

What is your experience now as you write about it?

_____

_____

Stay with process - What happened next?

_____

_____

Flexible attitude - Check assumptions

Did you have any expectations of what should or should not happen? If so, what were they? What happened?

_____

_____

Clarify its meaning

How did you understand what occurred, did you think about it or simply return to your breath?

_____

_____

Show genuine interest, kindness and compassion

Were there any particular times when you became aware of the need for kindness and compassion. If so, what happened?

_____

_____

What is the experience of kindness and compassion?

_____

_____

How curious were you in the experience of awarenessing? What helped you focus and be awake?

_____

_____

Being non-judging

Were you able to be kind to yourself if judging arose? How long did judging last if it occurred?

_____

_____

What was the physical expression of judging in your body?

_____

_____

Return to the present moment and ask what's happening now?

_____

_____

Not yesterday or the day before or before that.

Not tomorrow or what could happen in the future.

What is here to appreciate now?

_____

_____

RESPONDING: COPING AND MANAGING STRESS

Reading this book means you have already successfully navigated many of the challenges inherent in being human, being in school, learning to read, and problem-solving. Can you acknowledge this or do you take it for granted? How do you appraise your own ability to manage stress? What gets you going?

It takes a certain amount of time and concentration, as well as resources, to select a book, especially one that involves commitment to facing the self and celebrating the fullness of our lives, as well as opening into and facing its pain and loss. How wonderful to want to continue learning. Can this be appreciated as a strength? Too often, we take for granted our innate talents and capacity for growth.

Stop
Take a breath
Open, observe
Proceed

TAKE A MOMENT

Smile

Cherish the self that is sitting here now.

Name 5 things you appreciate in yourself

    1.

    2.

    3.

    4.

    5.

Is this pleasant, unpleasant or neutral? What is its effect?

Whether we believe we can cope or not makes a difference. It builds on past experience and creates future possibilities. Our perspective exists **now**, based on the evidence here in front of us and within us.

Studies show that a healthy response to stress fosters resilience, flexibility, nurturance, compassion, empathy, generosity, joy, and trust, as well as more rapid wound healing, hardiness, a robust immune system and a general sense of wellbeing. We will get upset but we recover faster.

One of my patients says she quotes her little girl who learned in school this expression, "You get what you get but don't get upset."

How wonderful when we can do that.

Suzanne Kobasa, a clinical psychologist, conducted some studies in the 1970s. She observed a group of executives who had similar levels of stress for a three-year period and examined their relationship to stressors. The group that experienced greater health had attitudes she labelled stress hardiness: the ability to see stress and difficulty as a challenge, be motivated to commit to meeting this challenge and possessing a strong internal locus of control - a *yes I can* attitude.

Another researcher, Anton Antonovsky, a professor of medical sociology in Israel, examined the relationship between one's orientation to life and one's health, named salutogenesis. He found that coherence was relevant to the manageability of stress: a sense of comprehensibility, manageability and meaning. Culture and conditioning play a large part in the manageability of stress. Each day new neurons are born and new neural connections are wired together. Change is possible. When we can pause and give ourselves the space to respond rather than react, the body returns to a state of homeostasis and allows for our thinking brain, the prefrontal cortex, to engage. Recent studies in neuroscience indicate that mindfulness supports activity in the prefrontal cortex, the area having to do with a sense of well-being and approach versus avoidance. It supports growth and regeneration of the grey matter in the hippocampus (area having to do with memory and learning) and in structures associated with self-awareness, compassion and introspection, as well as decreases the area in the amygdala that appraises anxiety and threat.

There is no one formula for coping with stress. Mindfulness shines a flashlight on mind and body bringing awareness to how we are responding *in the moment to our experience of the moment*. The sustainability of our attention and willingness to observe with an intention to learn rather than judge affects our ability to manage stress. Richard Lazarus and Susan Folkman, psychologists, looked at cognition and the perception and appraisal of an event that emphasized developing problem-, emotion-, and meaning-focused coping strategies.

Emotion-Focused - Learning self-regulating strategies such as tolerating impulses through mindfulness (in addictions work it is called urge surfing), taking a step back, reappraising an event, gaining support, altering attitude.

Problem-Focused - Breaking the problem down into workable pieces. Used when we feel we have control of the situation and can manage the source of the problem.

STORY: GOOD, BAD WHO KNOWS?

A farmer living sometime in the early 1900s with his family, a wife and son, is very hard working. He has enough for his family to survive and a little extra but is very dependent on his horse, his plow and the land that he owns. One day in the springtime when he is plowing a field for seeding new crops his horse breaks free of its reins and runs away. This is bad, there is no extra money to buy a new horse and his neighbors and family members can't afford to lend him another horse. They hear about his misfortune and come to express their sympathy.

"We are so sorry," they say to the farmer. *"This is so bad."*

The farmer thanks them for coming but says to them, *"Good. Bad. Who Knows?"* He continues to plow his field himself. His wife and son help, sometimes a friend comes by to assist. The hours are long. He rises earlier, ends later. It is slow going without his horse but he persists. Some weeks pass and one morning his horse returns and brings with it a whole herd of wild horses. *"Wow, this is wonderful, it's so good,"* his friends say. Again, the farmer thanks them for caring but says, *"Good, bad. Who knows?"*

Time passes and the farmer enjoys the horses. Sometimes he loans them out and everyone benefits. Sometime later the farmer's son is out in the barn grooming one of the new horses, a beautiful stallion, and the horse kicks him and the boy breaks his leg. This could be disastrous. There is no modern surgery and the boy could be crippled and not able to walk well or work in the field. Friends again come by and say how bad this is and the farmer repeats, *"Good, bad. Who knows?"*

Time passes; the boy recovers, but walks with a limp. War is declared and all the young men of the village are conscripted and have to go but not the son.

Good, bad. Who knows?

I always tell this story when the topic of stress reactions versus response and coping styles are discussed. I then ask, *"Has anyone here had something that was bad turn into something good? What was it?"*

Always, hands go up. Sometimes I hear about a divorce that at the time was terrible but led to much greater happiness. I have heard about layoffs, firings, even accidents. One woman described the dream house that she and her husband built after they retired that was hit by lightning and burned down within a month of their moving into it. She described telling the night clerk about this at the hotel where they were forced to go and the hotel clerk telling her how sorry he was to hear about this but that there was another person in the hotel whose house also burned down and she lost not only the house but her husband too.

As we heard this story, we were all silent feeling its horror. The woman went on to tell us how hearing about this other person woke her up to how fortunate she was and how grateful it made her feel.

"And it changed my life," she said. *"Ever since I have been so grateful for what I have. My whole world has changed."*

I don't recommend experiencing a catastrophe to maintain perspective but as a teacher of mine has said, *"Every day I remember being alive is enough."*

Enough.

STRESS AND COPING STRATEGIES

Name a stressor:

_____

_____

_____

How I coped with it: Emotion-Focused (What I said to myself):

_____

_____

_____

Write down some adjectives to describe how you appraised it. If it felt overwhelming, insurmountable or discouraging, how did that affect how you approached the stressor and what you did? Write it down.

_____

_____

_____

If you appraised it as challenging, what were its challenges? How did that affect how you approached the stressor and what you did? Write it down.

_____

_____

_____

Stop
Take a breath
Open, observe
Proceed

What is it like to allow what is?

_____

_____

_____

Read over what you have written and see if you would like to add or delete anything. Review and cross out any words that are self-critical or judgmental. What attitudes would be helpful to employ? Are there any stories, inspirational readings or sayings that are helpful? What are they?

_____

_____

_____

Problem-Solving: Name the problem and the steps you can take toward its resolution.

_____

_____

_____

Would you like to make any changes in these strategies? If so, write them down. Can you commit to these changes and believe them possible to accomplish?

_____

_____

_____

Using Expressive Therapies in Working with Stress

Writing can be a useful tool in accessing and releasing strong feelings, as can art. A person who attended the Mindfulness-Based stress reduction classes suffered a traumatic brain injury and was unable to follow the guided meditations in verbal form, but she was able to go to her breath and used one word or short phrase to calm. Her primary meditation, however, was creating art. She used all types of media, colored pencils, paint, Ink and even clay. The forms and colors emerged spontaneously and were an outlet for internal states, thoughts and feelings that could not be articulated verbally but needed expression and release. Releasing them onto the page was calming.

Allow yourself to connect to a stressor in your life and choose materials that are easy to work with such as colored pencils, crayons, or clay and allow a stressor to emerge in form onto the paper or material you are choosing to work with. Allow it to emerge spontaneously and let it form without thought or analysis. It can be as large or small as you like. Do it as quickly as you can, letting any feelings or thoughts that arise flow from inside you and emerge without censor on the page.

When you are finished, you can look at it and add any words or phrases that come to you. You can continue journaling if that is a medium you use for expression. You may do this as often as you like. Some people journal with images rather than words. All is fine.

COMMUNICATION

Session 6: The Commune in Communication: Joining with and Deeply Listening

After a formal meditation, I sometimes ask people to pause, look around the room and notice what they are noticing, including what may have changed since we began our meditation. Awareness is not static or a technique to do. Instead, it is a way of living that helps us listen to what is needed as it is needed and be able to act on this information in a constructive way. We are not always silent or moving slowly; we speak, we encounter challenges and we interact with others. Communication is continuous non-verbally or verbally. One of the causes of stress is a sense of isolation and separateness, but we are all part of the human condition and no one is truly alone.

> *"Say hello to your neighbor,"*
>> I sometimes ask the class as a reminder that we are in connection and part of a community.
>
> *"Listen to the sound of your voice saying hello and the felt sense of seeing and listening to your neighbor as you are greeting each other again."*
>> And then, since we've been sitting for a while, an invitation to listen to the body and stand or do some stretches and mindful movement.
>
> *"Always listening to what this moment calls for . . . to what is needed now."*

Then attendance is taken and we listen to each other again. I speak, but the connection between members of the class is non-verbal as we listen to each other and the tones of voice as they say, "here" and "present" as I say their names out loud. Body language indicates mood and feeling. It can be more powerful than words. What we say, how we say it in a respectful and caring interaction with another is mindfulness in action. Not speaking is also a communication. The space between, the pause, or silence has meaning as does avoiding a conversation and looking away.

I am always aware of the delicacy of maintaining motivation and committing to having mindfulness be integrated throughout the day.

Communication comes from the word commune, to join with. Why communicate? I ask the class. What is being communicated? How is it being communicated? How do you know that

111

what you communicate is being received correctly? What is your communication style? Are you assertive, passive, aggressive? Do you tend to avoid conflict or wrestle with it? What does your body language reflect? How aware are you of what you are saying, and its effect? Can you take in a compliment as readily as a criticism? As awareness grows, so does knowing where we place attention. Is the glass half-empty or half full? And how does this affect what we hear and say?

Communication Styles—Aggressive, Passive and Assertive

Aggressive

Imagine that you are being aggressive and move into the position you would take bringing awareness to your position in space and the relationship to the recipient of your anger. How does it feel in your body? What is the interplay between the sensations and thoughts that are present? What words were used? What was the feeling behind the words and the outcome of the aggression? How familiar is this to you? Can you think of a time someone has been aggressive to you? What was the outcome?

_____

_____

_____

_____

Passive

Describe situations that evoke this in you? How does it feel to be passive? What is a passive response? Can you sculpt it physically and bring awareness to the thoughts and feelings this evokes and the connecting sensations? What is the outcome? Is this familiar?

_____

_____

_____

_____

Assertive   Describe a time you've been assertive and let yourself move into the physical position that reflects this ability to disagree with another and yet be respectful and clear. How does that feel in the body? What thoughts are present? Feelings? What is the outcome? How familiar is this for you?

_____

_____

_____

_____

Home Practice

Allow yourself to focus on the emotions that accompany your communications today. S.T.O.P and note the physical stance that accompanies what you are feeling. Note your mode of expression verbally, the words you are using and the non-verbal, tone of voice, pacing, eye contact and position in relation to the other person. Is there reactivity or a modulated response. Note outcome.

Bring awareness to communications that are easy and those that are uncomfortable, paying particular attention to the position of the body and the resulting thoughts and feelings.

Practice being present.
Practice unconditional regard.

INTERPERSONAL MINDFULNESS -
MEDITATIVE AWARENESS WITH OTHERS

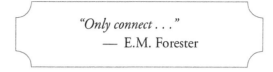

"Only connect . . ."
— E.M. Forester

From silence, awareness emerges and with it the ability for mindful communication. This is a relational practice that involves deep listening and speaking.

Gregory Kramer is the founder of Insight Dialogue from which interpersonal mindfulness was developed. On their website, www.metta.org is written, "the hungers for pleasure in relationships, to be seen or admired by others, and to hide or escape - these are all causes of suffering, which then are sustained by confusion and habit." This focus is relational as is the process of awarenessing through mindful communication. There is practice to:

- **Pause** - rest in the moment - letting go of the past and conditioned habits
- **Relax** - soften into and ease into what is being experienced
- **Open** - allow, being receptive and kind, no personal agenda
- **Trust Emergence** - accepting impermanence, faith in what arises, tranquility
- **Listen Deeply** - calm, seeking understanding
- **Speak the truth** - grounded in morality, mutuality and mindfulness

I recommend beginning the practice with some time to quiet the mind and give it space. As the mind settles, allow yourself to reflect on a source of suffering or an element that relieves suffering. Choose a subject for reflection that you would like to better understand. It can be the S.T.O.P., examining when and how to pause. It can be what is most valued and precious to you. Take your time to choose the subject and then invite another person who is also willing to pause, and practice mindful speaking with a willingness to relax, open, trust emergence, listen deeply, and speak the truth.

INTERPERSONAL MINDFULNESS

Choose a subject that you would like to explore and learn more about. It can be something challenging for you or an attitude or action you want to cultivate or strengthen.

- Decide who will speak first and who will listen.
- Speaker, using the guidelines above, has 5 minutes to speak freely and spontaneously on the agreed-upon subject uninterrupted.
- Listener pays attention with full mindfulness to what is being said and does not comment, fix or ask questions, but is silent bringing awareness internally to what arises as the speaker speaks.
- Pause
- Listener reflects back what was heard and experienced free of interpretation or comment (3min).
- Pause
- Switch and repeat above.
- After final pause, both people have an opportunity to speak together and reflect on the exchange.

In doing the exercise, you can also listen for content one time and reflect it back without interpretation or fixing. Another time, you can listen and report back on body language that is non-verbal.

THE ALL-DAY SESSION: PRACTICE - PRACTICE - MORE PRACTICE

Anxiety tends to be high immediately before this session. It is common for participants to be fearful as they enter the unknown, a whole day filled with silent meditation, sitting, walking, doing yoga, eating lunch and being present with the workings of body and mind. The day starts at 9:00 AM on a weekend day and ends at 4:00 PM. It is held after the sixth session, and there are two more sessions after it. The intention is to solidify and strengthen practice and experience the energy of a community coming together with a shared goal: Practicing Mindfulness.

Fear that they will freak out with all that quiet, fear they can't tolerate being still and worry that they will fail are common. Opening to and doing nothing but observing the workings of mind and its connection to body is scary. Accepting what arises, wishes and hurts, disappointments and successes, and observing their effect is challenging.

Pain patients don't know if they will be able to tolerate their pain even though time is spent discussing how they can care for themselves and receive permission to leave if necessary. People are told to dress in layers and bring pillows, blankets or mats so they can lie down if needed and to do yoga. Everyone who is attending the program is expected to come, and graduates of the program are also invited to join the day to refresh their practice.

No matter how many times I have led this day with my colleagues, I am moved. It is gutsy to plunge into the unknown of mindfulness, and the first time one does it formally for a full day demonstrates commitment and courage.

All the meditations that have been practiced in the classes are woven through the day beginning with some standing yoga and moving into a sitting meditation, more yoga, a body scan, active listening to a talk about practice from one of the teachers, silently eating lunch, a guided meditation on loving kindness, more sitting and walking, and, if weather permits, walking outside or resting, and then, as the day draws to an end, moving into mindful speech. This begins in a whisper in dyads and then enlarges to a small group of four and then opens to the whole room.

How was the day for you?
- Torture
- Amazing
- Peaceful
- I don't know

The day is not easily labelled or described, but what stands out is the pride in the accomplishment of having participated in it. Staying through the whole day is recognized as an achievement. There are many challenges. Pain, anxiety, boredom, restlessness, sometimes even flashbacks can happen. Some people are aware of having a choice in how to meet their challenge; others react automatically.

The length of the day provides sufficient time to be with the many moods and feelings that spontaneously arise and discover automatic reactions as well as more thoughtful responses to inner states. Watching the reaction or response to what occurs not only in mind but also viscerally in the body is a powerful learning. It is not academic but based on direct experience. There is time and support to practice leaning into aversion, refocusing and recovering. Balance is lost and balance regained.

Going home and re-entry is another challenge. After eight hours, the mind has quieted more than is realized, which increases sensitivity. If there is a feeling of calm and peace, the tendency is to want to hold on to it, but there is nothing to hold, only the motivation to continue practicing mindfulness. The stillness that has developed can be instantly challenged in the waiting line to pay the parking ticket or upon exiting the parking garage. Driving demands attention in another milieu as does returning home. **It is all an adventure.**

My Self-Retreat

Plan your own mindfulness session for either a half or full day. Let other people in your life know you are doing this and ask them to support your ability to take this time to nurture and care for yourself without having to be interrupted. Free yourself from obligations and responsibilities for this period.

Find a room or place where you can be undisturbed and that is a comfortable temperature making sure it is quiet and protected. Have handy a mat or blanket, a notebook and pencil if you choose to do some journaling, a pillow if needed and chair and meditation cushion. If you will be listening to a guided meditation have it available for easy use. You also may choose to have an inspirational reading.

In arranging the time make sure that other members in your living situation can support you and have it be a convenient time for all concerned. You might even do it with others with whom you share the practice of mindfulness. Below is a possible schedule for a morning self-retreat.

Date for the retreat _____

8:30–9:00 Prepare the room and have all needed supplies and materials

9:00–9:30 Yoga

9:30–10:00 Sitting Meditation (this order can be reversed, but alternate sitting with movement)

10:00–10:15 Walking Meditation

10:15–11:00 Guided Body Scan

11:00–11:30 Yoga/stretching

11:30–12:00 Sitting Meditation or Inspirational Reading

Lunch-rest-journaling

COMPASSION AND LOVING-KINDNESS MEDITATION

Being awake and aware means that we are open to pain and touch it with a gentle and tender heart. Traditionally, a loving-kindness meditation begins by sending wishes for well-being to self and then extending it out to others, first a loved one, then a person who does not evoke any strong feeling, usually a stranger you may have glanced at or nodded hello to but do not know, then a difficult person and finally to all beings everywhere. This includes the earth and all creatures on it. The words are very simple and can begin with a gatha like the one below by Thich Nhat Hahn,

> *"Breathing in I calm,*
> *Breathing out I smile.*
> *Dwelling in the present moment.*
> *It is a precious moment."*

Or a short prayer or line from a favorite poet that is inspirational.

In western culture, self-criticism is so endemic and conditioned it is often easier to begin this meditation by bringing into mind and heart the sense of a person we love rather than ourselves. It can be a clear image of the person in the mind's eye or a feeling sense. Sometimes it is even possible to hear their voice or remember their smell or touch, but what is most important is connecting to the feeling of love and the wish for them to be safe and protected, happy, healthy and free of suffering.

When you feel ready, time varies, there is no rush, just as you can give these wishes for well-being to another, allow yourself to receive them. Letting yourself embrace the being that is you and holding him or her to your heart, embracing this self as if he/she was a small child you were tending. You may do this for as long as you like. You may not experience the feelings behind the words you are saying.

The opposite is possible and sadness can arise, but don't stop. Think of this mediation as if you are cultivating a garden, nourishing it with good fertilizer, watering it and creating conditions that allow it to flourish. You may continue sending these wishes to yourself for as long as you like. Move on to another when there is a sense of fullness and you are ready.

Mindfulness includes compassion and loving-kindness. Below is a loving kindness meditation that you can practice. As you do it, notice what arises in you, treating yourself with the same sense of kindness and care that you can give and send to another. Use words that resonate with you and that you can connect to rather than repeating a phrase by rote that does not touch your heart/mind.

> *"May I be safe and protected.*
> *May I be happy.*
> *May I be healthy.*
> *May I live with ease."*

A Loving-Kindness Meditation

In doing this meditation, it is very important that you are as comfortable as possible and in a position that supports relaxation and ease. Doing this meditation has great benefits. It can help you experience joy and love within a sphere of safety and protection, helping you connect more intimately and authentically to yourself and to others.

Being loving and kind fosters compassion and understanding. It can sustain us in times of need. The more you can trust this process and allow yourself to receive the well wishes of this meditation, the more potent it will be.

Let your eyes close and allow yourself to relax. Notice the feelings in your body. Take a moment and be aware of any feelings or thoughts. Simply let them be and watch them go like clouds floating along in a vast, blue sky. And if you'd like, you can feel your breath moving in your body, a reminder that yes, you are here.

When you're ready, if you can, bring to mind an image of a person that you've experienced as being loving and kind, a benefactor to you, who easily evokes feelings of warmth and love. To this person you can direct these phrases:

> *"May you be happy.*
> *May you be healthy.*
> *May you be safe and protected.*
> *May you live with ease."*

It is important that you connect to the meaning of the phrases. Feel free to substitute words of your own that resonate with you. Do this for a period of time until you feel a sense of the wishes that you are sending forth. When you feel ready, you can give yourself these wishes for health and happiness, safety and ease of being.

Take as much time as you like. If your mind wanders, gently bring it back to the next phrase or repeat the one you had been saying. You can do this as often as you wish, adapting it to resonate with you, choosing words or phrases that have meaning for you that you can easily connect to as you say them to yourself. Take your time and say the phrases with love and intentionality. They may be repeated.

When you feel satisfied that you have fully sent these wishes for well-being and happiness to your benefactor, repeat them to yourself and give them to yourself freely without straining or feeling guilty. The more full we feel and the happier we are, the easier it is to radiate and reflect it out to others. Do this for as long as you want.

If you like, you can continue this meditation sending the wishes for safety and protection, mental and physical happiness and ease of being to people in your life who are neutral to you, people that you may only see occasionally or even strangers. Notice what arises as you do this.

When you feel this is complete, almost like a pool being filled with love and kindness, compassion and joy, you can then send these wishes to a difficult person. You can also send these wishes to parts of yourself that are hard for you to like and to accept. Do this with gentleness and care and only when you feel ready to do so.

And you can continue repeating phrases of loving-kindness to yourself and others as often as you like, adding pets, plants, nature, all living and non-living beings, visible and invisible. You can do this wherever you are; the important thing is to feel the connection between yourself and the phrases, saying them with an open heart, tenderly and compassionately.

Remember: be kind to yourself and no judging; you're allowing yourself to ask for what you need and receive these wishes, so you can be full and at peace. Then, you will be able to serve others as a beacon of peace and light.

We're all in this together. May we all be at peace.

Section 8

♡

Bringing Mindfulness Home

Taking Mindfulness Home - Sessions 7 & 8

When people return to class after practicing mindfulness for eight hours in the all-day session, there is often a renewed sense of purpose. This gives a boost to practice but also raises many questions about the self and patterns of thought. Participants discover that it is hard to bring awareness to body and mind throughout a whole day of mindfulness. Whatever is unsettled can come to the fore and leaning into and accepting what is perceived as aversive is challenging. Compassion and a steadiness of attention that is just beginning to be established is required.

The all-day session reinforces what has been practiced in class and gives more space, direction and time to observe, react and recover in the hope that this will be continued at home. As class moves toward ending, opportunities to recognize ruminations and drop old patterns of thought are discussed.

Refocusing and returning attention to the present moment and a neutral object like the breath is repeated in the last two classes and emphasized to incorporate into daily life. There is a greater sense of urgency to meet goals (feel better).

As the classes come to a conclusion, fear that mindfulness can't be sustained on their own is expressed. There is an appreciation of other class members and the support that is provided by shared experience. With this comes the realization that no one is alone and we all share the human condition.

People have received a taste of mindfulness. The challenge as classes end is how to ensure that this taste becomes daily nourishment. There has been the guidance of a teacher for protection, clarification and support; now each person must truly be their own coach and teacher. Many participants have experienced moving safely through anxiety or pain, as well as mind states. People have directly experienced the effect of their thinking - that they are not their thoughts. The challenge is to remember this.

Awareness is critical for regulating our emotions. It helps us reappraise our concept of self and allows us to catch the triggers of reactivity. As we grow up, we all learn ways of acting and thinking that form a story about who we think we are. Mindfulness allows us to observe the neural pathways that have been entrenched in our system, interrupt them, and lay down new ones.

The pause, the ability to S.T.O.P., interrupts these old patterns of thought and their resulting feelings. It makes room for new ways of responding to create new neural connections that are more constructive. As Frankl reminds us, the pause is where growth can occur.

The perceptual apparatus becomes broader, allowing for a more realistic appraisal of events and the intake of new, evidence-based facts. Change, however, can be scary, and recognizing old habits can evoke shame and fear. This feeds defensive states such as restlessness, boredom, aversion, sadness and yes, happiness and even peace.

Facing what is, with love and acceptance, goes beyond any formula or any one practice. Attending an eight-week program can inspire and give tools to use, but it is only a beginning of life-long learning. What are you doing/being is the focus of the last two classes as is how to continue bringing mindfulness into your life.

Much of the last two weeks of MBSR is consolidating practice and supporting its integration into daily life. *Remembering* to be mindful is helped by repetition Therefore, all the practices are reviewed and repeated in Sessions 7 and 8. Repetition is needed to lay down new neural pathways. Attention regulation is reinforced by *remembering* to return to direct experience NOW, as it is happening in body and mind.

In session seven, the discussion of the all-day session gives rise to many questions. By this time, class has become a community of people practicing honestly and authentically. Fears and longings are able to be recognized and named. Each person, in their own way, is struggling but working to face the truth of their lives as it is unfolding with greater clarity, kindness, and objectivity. This is helpful as one of the biggest questions is, "Am I doing it right? I still have . . . ."

Every time a person discovers their mind has wandered and is in default mode (distracted or ruminating) and returns their attention to an object, like the breath, I find myself saying, "Wonderful!" People are learning that they need not be at the mercy of their thoughts or automatic, conditioned reactions. Resting on the bank of the river rather than being in the stream of thoughts and feelings increases choice and a sense of control.

Recognizing trigger points lets us S.T.O.P to reexamine the validity of beliefs and the thoughts that support them. Pausing and stopping when the body is telling us it is contracted and reactive gives us the time and space to observe and evaluate what is needed and possible. It is empowering. Sustaining attention on a given object, usually breath, but whatever is neutral, and remembering to do it again and again is an ongoing practice. "What will help you continue to do this?" is the subject highlighted.

Mindfulness helps us be more awake, alert and effective in whatever we are doing but it requires sustained effort. The challenge is to sustain practice once class is over and the question is how.

HOW WILL YOU CONTINUE TO BRING MINDFULNESS INTO YOUR LIFE? WHAT HELPS YOU REMEMBER?

You Do Not Need To Be At The Mercy Of Your Thoughts
Mindfulness gives choices, control, modulation of emotions and greater range of response ability.

We Are More Than We Think We Are
Freer to be who we are based on fact rather than old stories and conditioning

We Can Approach Things In A Different Way
Able to cope more effectively with greater resilience and flexibility

Perspective Can Broaden And Change
Taking a step back and seeing with a clearer, less biased lens helps us get unstuck

Kindness Is Essential
Being more compassionate to self, accepting what we wish were different, helps and opens us to sharing the human condition

Sustaining Mindfulness

Formal Practice

1. Commit to a regular time for formal practice. Decide this in advance and you can even write it down in an appointment book or on an electronic calendar.

2. Decide on the length of time and set a timer.

3. Have a special place that is your spot for meditation or yoga that is safe, comfortable and protected.

4. Decide whether you will be doing a body scan, sitting meditation, walking meditation or yoga. If you need special supplies, earphones, CD, blanket, cushion or mat, have them accessible.

5. Communicate with family member(s) to enlist their cooperation and confirm that the time you take is OK with them and will be respected.

Renew Your Commitment And Write It Down

_____

_____

_____

Informal Practice

1. Every day, every moment, is an opportunity for practice. In the first session of the MBSR class, we offered a raisin to participants and asked them to examine it with a fresh perspective, as if they hadn't seen it before, and to digest it very slowly and mindfully. The home practice was to eat a portion of a meal in a similar way. It need not be a whole meal. It can be a forkful. It can be the care and attention given to cooking, even spaghetti. You might examine a vegetable or piece of fruit with eyes for shape and color, tap it with your fingers to test its firmness, if appropriate listen to how it sounds, bring it up to your nose and smell it and then either put it in your basket, bringing awareness to your internal command to do so and noting how that translates to shoulder, arm, hand and then at home placing it in the refrigerator or tasting it and beginning to eat it. This is one example, but there are myriad possibilities revolving around an ordinary and frequent activity that is routine.

2. Another example could be bringing awareness to waking up in the morning. What is the mood, your first thought, the feel of the pillow, the mattress, your body and how you get out of bed? What happens next?

3. Perhaps brushing your teeth or preparing a morning beverage can be chosen as an object of attention.

4. When you come home, what is the first thing you do? Note the entry into your home and have that be a time to be present to what greets you - and smile!

During the Day at Work

1. What is a repetitive activity that you do? Bring awareness to it and let it be a cue to S.T.O.P., have a time out to pause and refresh.

2. When you sit down to the computer, can this be a mindful moment before you turn it on?

3. When the urge to look at your cell phone arrives, can you take a breath?

4. When you hear the ting of a text being announced, can this be a mindful moment?

5. Please add to this list and post it in a visible place to help you remember to S.T.O.P. and be mindful.

6.

7.

8.

9.

10.

REMEMBER:

My intention:_____

My commitment:_____

And you can add a slogan for yourself to live by, inspirational sayings and quotes, books and pictures.

Examples:

• *Yes to life and all that's in it*
• *It's not dying that I worry about but how am I living now?*
• *Remember kindness*
• *I am worthy*

My sources of inspiration and slogans to live by:

_____

_____

_____

CONGRATULATIONS - YOU HAVE ARRIVED HERE

My Schedule of Meditation

Week of _____

	Monday	Tuesday	Wednesday	Thursday	Friday	Saturday	Sunday
Time & Type of Meditation							
Place							

Week of _____

	Monday	Tuesday	Wednesday	Thursday	Friday	Saturday	Sunday
Time & Type of Meditation							
Place							

Week of _____

	Monday	Tuesday	Wednesday	Thursday	Friday	Saturday	Sunday
Time & Type of Meditation							
Place							

Week of _____

	Monday	Tuesday	Wednesday	Thursday	Friday	Saturday	Sunday
Time & Type of Meditation							
Place							

Notes to Self

References, Resources and Recommendations

BOOKS

Begly, Sharon. (2007). *Train your Brain, Change your Mind*. New York: Ballantine Books.

Baer, Ruth. (2014). *Mindfulness based treatment approaches (second edition): The clinicians guide to evidence base and applications*. London: Elsevier.

Boone, M. S. (2014). *Mindfulness and Acceptance in Social Work: Evidence-based interventions and emerging applications*. Oakland, CA: New Harbinger Publications.

Brewer, Jud. (2017). *The Craving Mind*. Yale University Press.

Competence in Teaching Mindfulness-Based Courses: Concepts, Development and Assessment. Crane, Kuyken, Williams, Hastings, Cooper & Fennell, 2012.

Cappy, Peggy. (2006). *Yoga for All of Us: A modified series of traditional poses for any age and ability*. New York: St. Martin's Press. [Also see Peggy Cappy DVDs for yoga adaptation.]

Cullen, M. & Brito, G. (2015). *The Mindfulness-Based Emotional Balance Workbook: An Eight Week Program for Improved Emotion Regulation and Resilience*. Oakland: New Harbinger.

Fabrizio, Didonna. (2009). *Clinical Handbook of Mindfulness*. Springer.

Fischer, Norman. (2012). *Training in Compassion*. Shambhala, Boston.

Germer, Christopher. (2009). *The Mindful Path to Self-Compassion*. Guilford Press, New York.

Germer, C. K., Siegel, R. D., & Fulton, P. R. (2013). *Mindfulness and Psychotherapy: Second edition*. New York: Guilford.

Greenland, Susan Kaiser. (2016). *Mindful Games*. Shambhala, Boulder.

Hayes, S. C., Follette, V. M. & Linehan, M. M. (Eds.). (2004). *Mindfulness and acceptance: Expanding the cognitive–behavioral tradition*. New York: Guilford Press.

Hick, S. F. (Ed.). (2009). *Mindfulness and Social Work*. Chicago: Lyceum.

Kabat-Zinn, J. (1994). *Wherever you go, there you are: Mindfulness meditation in everyday life*. New York: Hyperion.

Kabat-Zinn, J. (2013). *Full Catastrophe Living (Revised Ed.)*. New York: Bantam Books.

Kramer, Gregory. (2007). *Insight Dialogue*. Shambhala, Boston.

Kristeller, Jean. (2015). *The Joy of Half a Cookie*. A Perigee Book.

Linehan, M. M. (1993a). *Cognitive-behavioral treatment of borderline personality disorder*. New York: Guilford Press.

Linehan, M. M. (1993b). *Skills training manual for treating borderline personality disorder.* New York: Guilford Press.

McBee, L. (2008). *Mindfulness Based Elder Care.* New York: Springer.

McCown, D., Reibel, D. K., Micozzi, M. S. *(2010). Teaching Mindfulness.* Springer

Neff, Kristin. (2011). *Self-Compassion.* Harper Collins

Peltz, Lawrence. (2013). *The Mindful Path to Addiction Recovery.* Trumpeter.

Pollak, Susan, Pedulla, Thomas, & Siegel, Ronald. (2014). *Sitting Together.* Guilford.

Ram, Dass. (2000). *Still Here, Embracing Aging, Changing, and Dying.* New York: Riverhead Books.

Remen, Rachel Naomi. (1996). *Kitchen Table Wisdom.* New York: Riverhead.

Rosenbaum, Elana. (2005). *Here for Now: Living Well with Cancer through Mindfulness.* New York: Satya House.

Rosenbaum, Elana. (2012). *Being Well (even when you're sick): Mindfulness Practices for People Living with Cancer And Other Serious Illnesses.* Boston: Shambhala.

Rosenbaum, Robert, & Magid, Barry. (2016). *What's Wrong with Mindfulness (and what isn't).* Wisdom Publications, Boston.

Salzberg, S. (2004). *Lovingkindness: The revolutionary art of happiness.* Shambala.

Santorelli, Saki.(1999). *Heal Thy Self, Lessons on Mindfulness in Medicine.* Bell Tower, New York, NY.

Sapolsky, R. (2004). *Why zebras don't get ulcers (Third Ed.).* New York: Holt Paperbacks.

Sears, D., Tirch, D., & Denton, R,(2011). *Mindfulness in Clinical Practice.* Professional Resource Press.

Sears, Richard W. (2014). *Mindfulness: Living through Challenges and Enriching Your Life in This Moment.* Wiley & Sons.

Segal, Z. V., Williams, J. G., & Teasdale, J. D. (2003). *Mindfulness-Based cognitive therapy for depression: Second edition.* New York: The Guilford Press.

Shapiro, S. L. & Carlson, L. E. (2009). *The Art and Science of Mindfulness: Integrating mindfulness into psychology and the helping professions.* Washington, DC: American Psychological Association.

Siegel, Ronald D. (2009). *The Mindfulness Solution.* Guilford Press.

Stahl, Robert, Goldstein, Elisha, & Kabat-Zinn, Jon. (2010). *MBSR Workbook,* New Harbinger.

Stahl, B., Meleo-Meyer, F., & Koerbel, L. (2014), *A Mindfulness-Based Stress Reduction Workshop for Anxiety.* New Harbinger.

Teasdale, John, Williams, Mark, & Segal, Zindel. (2014). *The Mindful Way Workbook.* Guilford Press.

van der Kolk, B. (2014). *The Body Keeps Score: Brain, mind, and body in the healing of trauma.* New York: Viking Penguin.

Willard, Christopher. (2010). *Child's Mind.* Parallex Press, Berkeley.

Willard, Christopher. (2016). *Growing Up Mindful: Essential Practices to Help Children, Teens, and Families Find Balance, Calm and Resilience.* Sounds True.

Williams, Mark, & Kabat-Zinn, Jon. (2013). *Mindfulness: Diverse Perspectives on its Meaning, Origins and Applications.* Routledge.

SELECTED RESEARCH

Kabat-Zinn, J. (2011, May). Some Reflections on the Origins of MBSR, Skillful Means and the Trouble with Maps. *Contemporary Buddhism*, Vol. 12, No. 1.

Garrison, K. M. and Brewer, J. A. "Quieting the mind: meditation leads to decreased activation in self-referential nodes of the default mode network beyond general task-based deactivation." (under review). *Center for Mindfulness in Medicines, Health Care, and Society.*

Brewer, J. A. (2014). "Mindfulness in the Military." *Am. J. Psychiatry, 171*: 803-6.

Garrison, K. M., Scheinost, D., Constable, R. T., and Brewer, J. A. "Neural activity and functional connectivity of loving kindness meditation." *Brain and Behavior,* PMC: 4(3) 337-347. open access journal.

Brewer, J. A. Garrison, K. M., and Whitfield-Gabrieli, S. (2013) "What about the 'self' is processed in the posterior cingulate cortex?" *Frontiers in Human Neuroscience, 7*: 647.

Garrison, K. M., Santoyo, J. F., Davis, J. H., Thornhill IV, T. A., Thompson, Kerr, C. E., Brewer, J. A. (2013) "Effortless awareness: using real-time neurofeedback to probe correlates of posterior cingulate cortex activity in meditators' self-report." *Frontiers in Human Neuroscience, 7*: 440.

Holzel, B. K., Lazar, S. W., Gard, T., Schuman-Oliver, Z., Vago, D. R., Ott, U. (2011, October). "How Does Mindfulness Meditation Work? Proposing Mechanisms of Action From a Conceptual and Neural Perspective". *Perspectives on Psychological Science, 6*(6)537-559, http://pps.sagepu

Schuman-Olivier, Z., Hoeppner, B. B., Evins, A. E., Brewer, J. A. (2014, April). "Finding the right match: Mindfulness training may potentiate the therapeutic effect of nonjudgment of inner experience on smoking cessation." *Substance Use and Misuse,* 49(5): 586-94.

Brewer, J. A. and Garrison, K. M. (2014, January). "The posterior cingulate cortex as a plausible mechanistic target of meditation: Findings from neuroimaging." *Annals of N Y Acad Sci,* 1307: 19-27.

Garrison, K. A., Scheinost, D., Worhunsky, P. D., Elwafi, H. M., Thornhill IV, T. A., Thompson, E., Saron, C., Desbordes, G., Kober, H., Hampson, M., Gray, J. R., Constable, R. T., Papademetris, X., Brewer, J. A. (2013, November). "Real-time fMRI links subjective experience with brain activity during focused attention." *NeuroImage,* 81:110-118.

Elwafi, H. M., Witkiewitz, K., Mallik, S., Thornhill IV, T. A., Brewer, J. A. (2013, June). "Mechanisms of mindfulness training in smoking cessation: moderation of the relationship between craving and cigarette use." *Drug and Alcohol Dependence,* 130(1-3): 222-29.

Brewer, J. A., Davis, J. H., Goldstein, J. (2013, March). "Why is it so hard to pay attention, or is it? Mindfulness, the factors of awakening and reward-based learning." *Mindfulness,* 4(1).

Brewer, J. A., Elwafi, H. M., Davis, J. H. (2013, June). "Craving to Quit: psychological models and neurobiological mechanisms of mindfulness training as treatment for addictions." *Psychology of Addictive Behaviors,* 27(2):366-79.

Libby, D. J., Worhunsky, P. D., Pilver, C. E., Brewer, J. A. (2012, March). "Meditation-induced changes in high-frequency heart rate variability predict smoking outcomes." *Frontiers in Human Neuroscience,* 6:54.

Brewer, J. A., Worhunsky, P. D., Gray, J. R., Tang, Y. Y., Weber, J., Kober, H. (2011, December). "Meditation experience is associated with differences in default mode network activity and connectivity." *Proceedings of the National Academy of Sciences of the United States of America,*13;108(50).

Brewer, J. A., Mallik, S., Babuscio, T. A., Nich, C., Johnson, H. E., Deleone, C. M., Minnix-Cotton, C. A., Byrne, S. A., Kober, H., Weinstein, A. J., Carroll, K. M., Rounsaville, B. J. (2011, December). "Mindfulness Training for smoking cessation: results from a randomized controlled trial." *Drug and Alcohol Dependence,* 1;119,(1-2): 72-80.

Brewer, J. A., Bowen, S., Smith, J. T., Marlatt, G. A., Potenza, M. N. (2010, October). "Applying Mindfulness-Based Treatments to Co-Occurring Disorders: What Can We Learn From the Brain?" *Addiction,* 105(10): 1698-1706.

Brewer, J. A., Sinha, R., Chen, J. A., Michalsen, R. N., Babuscio, T. A., Nich, C., Grier, A., Bergquist, K. L., Reis, D. L., Potenza, M. N., Carroll, K. M., Rounsaville, B. J. (2009, Oct-Dec). "Mindfulness Training and Stress Reactivity in Substance Abuse: Results from A Randomized, Controlled Stage I Pilot Study." *Substance Abuse,* 30 (4): 306-17.

Brewer, J. A., Grant, J. E., and Potenza, M. N. (2008, March). "The Treatment of Pathologic Gambling." *Addictive Disorders and Their Treatment,* 7(1): 1-13.

Brewer, J. A. and Potenza, M. N. (2008, January). "The neurobiology and genetic of impulse control disorders: Relationships to drug addictions." *Biochemical Pharmacology,* 75(1): 63-75.

Brewer, J. A., Worhunsky, P. D., Carroll, K. M., Rounsaville, B. J., Potenza, M. N. (2008, December). "Pre-Treatment Brain Activation During Stroop Task is Associated with Treatment Outcomes in Cocaine Dependent Patients." *Biological Psychiatry,* 1;64(11): 998-1004.

Grant, J., E., Brewer, J. A., Potenza, M. N. (2006, December). "Neurobiology of Substance and Behavioral Addictions." *CNS Spectrums* 11(12):924-30.

The American Mindfulness Research Association, www.goamra.org - Monthly database for mindfulness research.

SELECTED ARTICLES

Barnes, N., Hattan, P., Black, D., Schuman-Olivier, Z. (2016, October). An Examination of Mindfulness-Based Programs in US Medical Schools. *Mindfulness,* (DOI 10.1007/s12671-016-0623-8)

Crane, R. S., Kuyken, W., Williams, J. M. G., Hastings, R. P., Cooper, L., & Fennell, M. J. V. (2012, March).Competence in Teaching Mindfulness-Based Courses: Concepts, Development and Assessment. *Mindfulness* 3(1); 76-84.

Epstein, R. M. & Back, A. L. (2015). Responding to suffering. *JAMA,* 314(24):2623-2626.

Epstein, R. M. (1999, September). Mindful Practice. *JAMA,* 1;282(9):833-839.

Geiger, P.J., Boggero, I. A., Brake, C. A., Caldera, C.A., Combs, H. L., Peters, J. R. & Baer, R. A. (2016, April). Mindfulness-Based Interventions for Older Adults: a Review of the Effects on Physical and Emotional Well-Being. *Mindfulness,* 7(2):296-307.

Hofmann, S. G., Grossman, P. & Hinton, D. E. (2011, November). Loving-kindness and compassion meditation: Potential for psychological interventions. *Clinical Psychology Review,* 31(7):1126–1132.

Kallapiran, K., Koo, S., Kirubakaran, R., & Hancock, K. (2015). Review: Effectiveness of mindfulness in improving mental health symptoms of children and adolescents: a meta-analysis. *Child and Adolescent Mental Health,* 20(4), 182-194.

Keng, S. L., Smoski, M. J., Robins, C. J. (2011, August). Effects of Mindfulness on Psychological Health: A Review of Empirical Studies. *Clin Psychol Rev,* 31(6):1041-1056.

Khoury, B., Lecomte, T., Fortin, G., Masse, M., Therien, P., Bouchard, V., Chapleau, M-A., Paquin, K. & Hofmann, S. G. (2013, August). Mindfulness-Based therapy: A comprehensive meta-analysis. *Clinical Psychology Review,* 33(6):763-771.

Killingsworth, M. A., & Gilbert, D. T. (2010, November). A wandering mind is an unhappy mind. *Science,* 330(6006):932.

Mani, M., Kavanagh, D. J., Hides, L., Stoyanov. S. R. (2015, August). Review and Evaluation of Mindfulness-Based iPhone Apps. *Journal of Medical Internet Research,* 19;3(3):e82.

Pilkington, K., Kirkwood, G., Rampes, H. & Richardson, J. (2005, December). Yoga for depression: The research evidence. *Journal of Affective Disorders,* 89(1-3):13-24.

Strauss, C., Thomas, N. & Hayward, M. (2015, August). Can we respond mindfully to distressing voices? A systematic review of evidence for engagement, acceptability, effectiveness and mechanisms of change for Mindfulness-Based interventions for people distressed by hearing voices. *Frontiers in Psychology,* 14;6:1154.

Trowbridge, K. & Lawson, L. (2016). Mindfulness-Based interventions with social workers and the potential for enhanced patient-centered care: A systematic review of the literature. *Social Work Health Care,* 55(2):101-24.

van der Kolk, B. A. (2006, July). Clinical implications of neuroscience research in PTSD. *Annals of N Y Academy of Sciences,* 1071:277-293.

Yang, Y., Liu, Y., Zhang, H. & Liu, J. (2015, September). Effectiveness of Mindfulness-Based stress reduction and Mindfulness-Based cognitive therapies on people living with HIV: A systematic review and meta-analysis. *International Journal of Nursing Sciences,* 2:3:283–294.

Ying, Y. W. (2009). Contribution of self-compassion to competence and mental health in social work students. *Journal of Social Work Education, 45*(2): 309-323.

WEBLINKS

Mindful Magazine
http://www.mindful.org/magazine/

The Center for Mindfulness, University of Massachusetts Medical Center
https://www.umassmed.edu/cfm/

The Center for Mindfulness and Compassion
www.chacmc.org

The Center for Compassion and Altruism Research and Education
http://ccare.stanford.edu/

The National Center for Complementary and Alternative Medicine
https://nccih.nih.gov/

The Dhamma Brothers
http://www.dhammabrothers.com/

Mindfulness and compassion for vets with PTSD: Healing a soldier's heart
http://www.seattlechannel.org/CommunityStories?videoid=x23995

The Institute for Mediation and Psychotherapy
http://www.meditationandpsychotherapy.org/

Elana's Website
http://www.mindfuliving.com/

Online material and recordings of mindfulness practices and related teachings

https://www.gaia.com/
web-based yoga classes plus more

http://www.dharmaseed.org/
free offerings of western Buddhist teachers talks

http://www.dharma.org/
Insight Meditation (retreats, classes and podcasts)

https://soundcloud.com/buddhistgeeks
Soundcloud: Search for artists, bands, tracks, podcasts

https://www.betterlisten.com/
Listen, Learn, Live – Better!

http://mindfulness-solution.com/
Everyday Practices for Everyday Problems

https://metta.org/
Teachings from Insight Dialogue

http://www.soundstrue.com/store/
Recordings from mindfulness meditation teachers

http://www.audiodharma.org/
Talks from mindfulness teachers

APPS

Some Guided Mindfulness Recordings

All available online for free at:

1. UCLA Mindful Awareness Research Center
   Guided Mindfulness Practices
   http://marc.ucla.edu/body.cfm?id=22

2. UC San Diego Center for Mindfulness Website
   Guided Mindfulness Practices
   http://health.ucsd.edu/specialties/mindfulness/programs/mbsr/Pages/audio.aspx

3. Sitting Together Website
   Guided Mindfulness and Compassion Practices
   http://sittingtogether.com/meditations.php

4. Center for Mindful Self-Compassion Website
   Guided Compassion and Self-Compassion Practices
   http://www.centerformsc.org/meditations

5. Tara Brach Website
   Guided Practices
   http://www.tarabrach.com/audioarchives-guided-meditations.html

Popular Mindfulness Apps

Headspace
Free app for iPhone and Android
https://www.headspace.com/

Insight Timer
Free app for iPhone and Android
https://insighttimer.com/

Stop, Breathe & Think
Free app for iPhone, Android, and Web
http://www.stopbreathethink.org/

Buddhify
For iOS and Android
http://buddhify.com/

Calm
Meditation Techniques for Sleep and Stress Reduction
https://www.calm.com/

Omvana
Free app for iPhone and Android
http://www.omvana.com/

The Mindfulness App
http://www.themindfulnessapp.com/

Smiling Mind
https://smilingmind.com.au/

Take a Break for Stress Relief
https://itunes.apple.com/us/app/take-break!-guided-meditations/id453857236?mt=8

The Mindfulness Training App
Free app for iPhone
https://itunes.apple.com/us/app/themindfulness-training-app/id687853790?mt=8

Eat Right Now® - A simple way to develop healthy eating habits
https://goeatrightnow.com/

Smoking Cessation
http://www.mindful.org/craving-to-quit/

Listing of Buddhist meditation centers worldwide
http://www.buddhanet.info/wbd/